POWER STUDIES 3

CONTENTS

Page   **Audio Track**

Page		Track
2	Introduction	
3	Foreword	
4	Power Studies 3 Bonus Song List	
	Introduction To The Recording	1
	Tuning	2
5	People Get Ready *Jeff Beck*	3
12	The Sunshine Of Your Love *Cream*	4
	E♭ Tuning	5
20	Sweet Child O' Mine *Guns N' Roses*	6
31	Lenny *Stevie Ray Vaughan*	7
40	Hideaway *Blues Breakers (John Mayall with Eric Clapton)*	8
47	Crazy Train *Ozzy Osbourne*	9
56	Black Magic Woman *Santana*	10
62	Reelin' In The Years *Steely Dan*	11
75	Another Brick In The Wall, Part 2 *Pink Floyd*	12
80	Iron Man *Black Sabbath*	13
87	You Shook Me *Led Zeppelin*	14
95	Glossary	

HAL•LEONARD CORPORATION

7777 W. BLUEMOUND RD. P.O. BOX 13819 MILWAUKEE, WI 53213

Copyright © 1994 by HAL LEONARD CORPORATION
International Copyright Secured   All Rights Reserved

For all works contained herein:
Unauthorized copying, arranging, adapting, recording or public performance is an infringement of copyright.
Infringers are liable under the law.

POWER STUDIES 3

INTRODUCTION

The *Power Studies* series is designed to bring you countless hours of musical enjoyment while enhancing the learning process and building your chops. In *Power Studies*, you are presented with an exciting array of your favorite songs to hone your musicianship and supplement the concepts in the *Wolf Marshall Guitar Method*. This will provide you with a meaningful environment for applying the method ideas while developing a working repertoire. An environment which is stimulating and fun—in the context of real music.

Through the music itself, you will experience and assimilate the same powerful ideas that have inspired all the great guitarists from Jimi Hendrix and Eric Clapton to Stevie Ray Vaughan and Edward Van Halen. The *Power Studies* material is a varied collection embracing many styles of music while focusing on a tight core of must-know tunes. Besides the emphasis on rock classics you'll explore different styles like rockabilly, blues, fusion, country, heavy metal and pop. Each *Power Studies* song is purposefully selected to reflect and amplify the important guitar playing principles found in your corresponding *Wolf Marshall Guitar Method*. You will get to know the music on a very intimate level.

Every song is preceded by a full annotation and performance notes which amount to a complete guitar lesson in their own right. These sections are filled with musical insights and shed light on the important technical points within each composition. You'll learn about the professional application of chords, scales, articulations, song form, rhythm playing, arpeggios and much more. Above all, *Power Studies* is dedicated to you—playing, hearing and understanding the music you love.

THE RECORDING

The recording for this book contains all of the songs from the book in complete musical settings. The featured guitar part (found in gray box areas in the book) is on the right channel, the rest of the instrumentation is on the left channel. The use of the gray box areas is not employed in songs where there is only one guitar part featured. Most of the time, the featured part contains material that explores the concepts and techniques taught in *Basics 3* of the *Wolf Marshall Guitar Method*. Occasionally, when there is only one guitar in an arrangement, the featured guitar part may go beyond the *Basics 3* level.

Wolf Marshall — guitars
Gary Ferguson — drums, percussion
Michael Della Gala — bass
John Nau — keyboards
Warren Hamm — harmonica on "You Shook Me"
Michael McCarty — additional sythesizer, percussion & engineer
Produced by Wolf Marshall

FOREWORD

In preparing these *Power Studies*, one naturally faces the dilemma of finding the ideal songs as musical illustrations to support the various teaching points as they are presented in *Basics 3*. However songs don't always cooperate with authors. They are living, breathing musical entities which yield techniques and theory only after existing as art. And that's as it should be.

With that said, there seemed two ways to approach the matter. One was to present only the pieces of a song which reflected the "letter of the lesson." In other words, omitting sections beyond the immediate scope of a lesson to satisfy teaching criteria alone. This approach would result in butcheries like songs without solos and often without some of their most significant riffs. Can you imagine "Crazy Train" without its immortal Randy Rhoads solo? Or Guns N' Roses "Sweet Child O' Mine" minus the signature wide interval intro? Unthinkable. Instead an alternate route was chosen. In the *Power Studies* series you play the entire song with all its parts intact to form a complete musical picture.

In the performance notes at the beginning of each song you will find points which are cross-referenced to other *Wolf Marshall Guitar Method* volumes. For example, references to certain lead guitar scales and ideas from *Advanced Concepts and Techniques* as well *Basics 1* and *2*, may be cited in the performance notes of *Power Studies 3*. These will aid you in not only selecting the particular "graded" parts to play within the *Power Studies 3* course, but will provide the advancing guitarist with a continuum of music throughout the *Power Studies* series.

By presenting each song in its entirety, complete with annotations, each volume of the series is as viable and valuable as the next and consequently no vital step in your musical growth will be overlooked or slighted. There is another benefit. The extra motivation it takes an aspiring guitarist to rise above his present abilities and struggle to learn a trickier scale fingering or that more difficult chord may well be what makes him a dedicated player and ultimately a successful musician. In this spirit I can truly say that this series lives up to its name—*Power Studies!*

Wolf Marshall

POWER STUDIES 3 BONUS SONG LIST

The following pieces can be used to expand and enhance your exploration of the major and minor pentatonic scale forms and chord shapes covered in Power Studies 3. Use the basic guidelines mentioned in the performance notes for "Lenny". As you work thru the riffs and solo phrases in the bonus list, assign a corresponding chord form to every line you learn. Don't forget to relate forms to the chords as well.

1. Little Wing—Jimi Hendrix/Stevie Ray Vaughan
2. Let It Be—The Beatles
3. Electric Eye—Judas Priest
4. Funk #49—James Gang
5. Jessica—The Allman Brothers Band
6. While My Guitar Gently Weeps—The Beatles/Jeff Healey
7. The Sky is Crying—Stevie Ray Vaughan
8. Born Under a Bad Sign—Albert King/Cream/Robben Ford
9. Rock and Roll Hoochie Koo—Johnny Winter
10. Free Bird—Lynyrd Skynyrd
11. Livin' on a Prayer—Bon Jovi
12. Layla—Derek and the Dominoes/Eric Clapton
13. Kid Charlemagne—Steely Dan
14. The End—The Beatles
15. More Than a Feeling—Boston
16. Dream On—Aerosmith
17. Change It—Stevie Ray Vaughan
18. All Along the Watchtower—Jimi Hendrix
19. All Your Love—Otis Rush/Eric Clapton/Gary Moore
20. Highway Star—Deep Purple
21. Stairway to Heaven—Led Zeppelin
22. Can't Get Enough—Bad Company
23. You're No Good—Van Halen
24. Still Got the Blues—Gary Moore
25. Time—Pink Floyd
26. Flying High Again—Ozzy Osbourne
27. Hotel California—Eagles
28. Paradise City—Guns N' Roses
29. Love Gun—Kiss
30. Wheel in the Sky—Journey
31. 21st Century Schizoid Man—King Crimson
32. Waiting For An Alibi—Thin Lizzy
33. Back in the Saddle—Aerosmith
34. See See Rider—Elvis Presley
35. Shapes of Things—Yardbirds/Jeff Beck/Gary Moore
36. Spanish Castle Magic—Jimi Hendrix
37. Only You Can Rock Me—UFO
38. Steppin' Out—Eric Clapton
39. Good Times, Bad Times—Led Zeppelin
40. If 6 Was 9—Jimi Hendrix
41. Mr. Brownstone—Guns N' Roses
42. Boys Are Back in Town—Thin Lizzy
43. Whole Lotta Love—Led Zeppelin
44. War Pigs—Black Sabbath
45. Back in Black—AC/DC
46. Black Dog—Led Zeppelin
47. Purple Haze—Jimi Hendrix
48. Carry On Wayward Son—Kansas
49. Photograph—Def Leppard
50. See the Light—Jeff Healey
51. Too Rolling Stoned—Robin Trower
52. Train Kept A Rollin'—Aerosmith
53. Crossfire—Stevie Ray Vaughan
54. Somebody Get Me a Doctor—Van Halen
55. You Shook Me All Night Long—AC/DC
56. Hound Dog—Elvis Presley
57. Since I've Been Loving You—Led Zeppelin
58. Blue Sky—The Allman Brothers Band
59. Hell Bent for Leather—Judas Priest
60. No One Like You—Scorpions

PEOPLE GET READY
Jeff Beck

Universally acclaimed as one of rock's premier and most influential guitarists, Jeff Beck has led many self-titled groups over the years but few as memorable as the all-star late-1960's lineup on *Truth* and *Beck-O-La* which debuted singer Rod Stewart. In 1985, Beck rejoined forces briefly with Stewart on the *Flash* album to produce one of the all-time great moments in the genre. "People Get Ready" is a cover of the Impressions' (Curtis Mayfield) 1965 gospel-tinged R&B hit reinterpreted with Rod's gravel-like vocals and Jeff's bluesy and haunting guitar lines. As the producer, he played it simple on this track using a direct-into-the-board Scholz Rockman for all the guitar parts and a sparse, synth-generated background as the canvas for his colorful soundscapes.

A short, unaccompanied chordal intro begins the piece [A]. In this intro as well as in the overall rhythm guitar part, Jeff uses a variety of both common and slightly unusual voicings. (The basic shapes can all be found in *Basics 3* in either their open or bar chord versions. The important D/F♯ inversion, for instance, is found on pg. 51). Note Beck's thumb fretting (designated with a T) of this and the G and G/A chords in the opening section. (For other significant examples of thumb fretting see Hendrix's "Hey Joe" in *Power Studies 2*). The recurring chord progressions labeled Rhy. Fig. 1 and Rhy. Fig. 2 are idiomatic to R&B and gospel music. These are constructed of simple changes using chords which are diatonic or in the key center of D. See the numerals below the TAB for their harmonic identity and function. For example, the D–Bm–G–D, Bm–Em–G/A–D will be designated by the numerals I–iii–IV–I and vi–ii–V–I

In his soloing, Jeff plays over both progressions elegantly, outlining the changes with strong sense of melodic continuity. He sticks primarily to the open G form (*Basics 3*: Ch. 1) often combined with the open E form (*Basics 3*: Ch. 4)—a standard connection in rock, blues, pop and country lead guitar styles. This combination of G and E forms of the major pentatonic is pursued throughout the intro [A] and first solo [D]. Note the tasteful addition of the 4th, G, to the otherwise straight pentatonic framework.

In the second solo [G], two more forms are added. Besides G and E forms, you'll find use of the open C form (*Basics 3*: Ch. 2) and the open A form (*Basics 3*: Ch. 3). (See *Basics 3*: Ch. 6, Connecting Major Forms, for more information.) Jeff's playing in these sections serves as further testimony to the major pentatonic's melodic nature and reveals how a scale in the hands of a skillful and imaginative master becomes a great artistic statement with attractive phrasing and interesting note choices. His single-note lines are beautiful examples of major pentatonic usage both as pure melody and as related to chords. Be sure to check out each phrase for strong note-to-chord relationships—a primary theme throughout *Basics 3*.

The song's signature motif, heard between sections, is an intervallic line (built on fourths and fifths) created by arpeggiating a D5 or E♭5 chord. (See arpeggiation in the beginning of *Basics 3*: Chapters 1–5.)

Also noteworthy in "People Get Ready" are the fills behind and around the vocal in the verses and the legendary Beck vibrato bar phrasing throughout.

End Rhy. Fig. 3
Gtr. 3: w/Rhy. Fig. 3
Ab/Bb
Eb
Cm7
Ab
8va
w/bar
full
Fm7
D
5 fr
P.H.
(8va)
P.M.
slow bend
I'm getting
H Outro
ready.
Gtr. 3: w/Rhy. Fig. 3, 1st 7 bars
Gtr. 2: w/Fill 1, 3 times
Gtr. 1
*mf
*Eb on 3rd stg. muted heavily w/fret hand.
Fill 1
Gtr. 2
(Distortion)
T
A
B

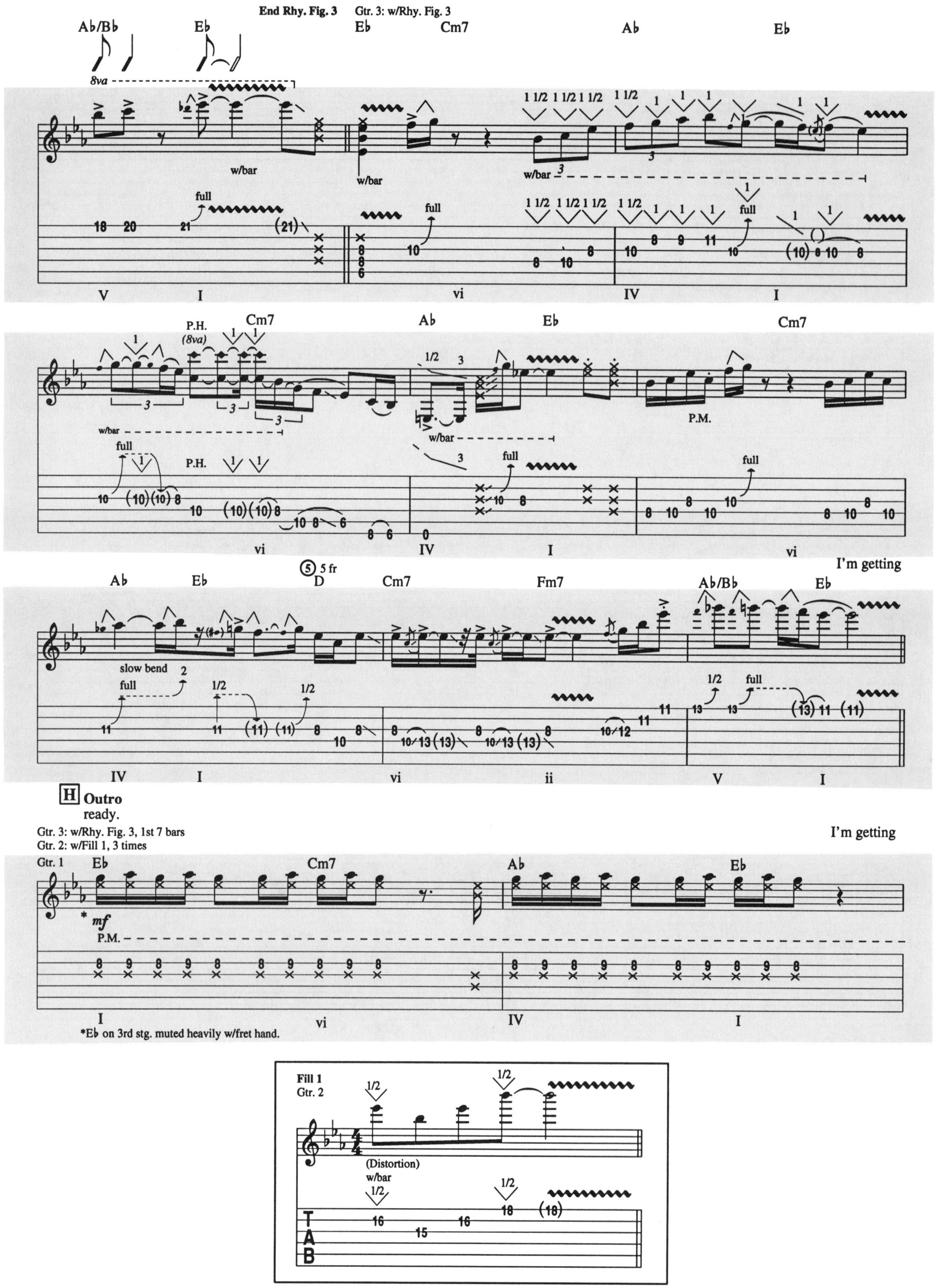

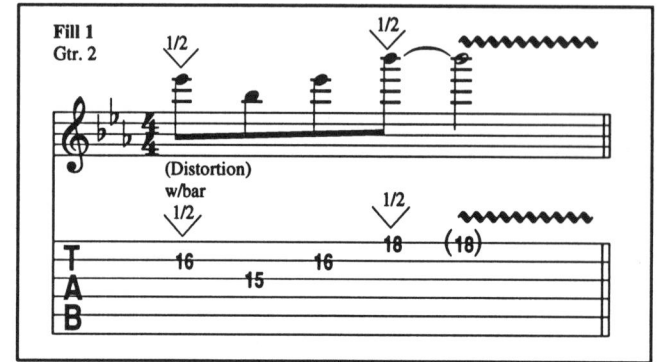

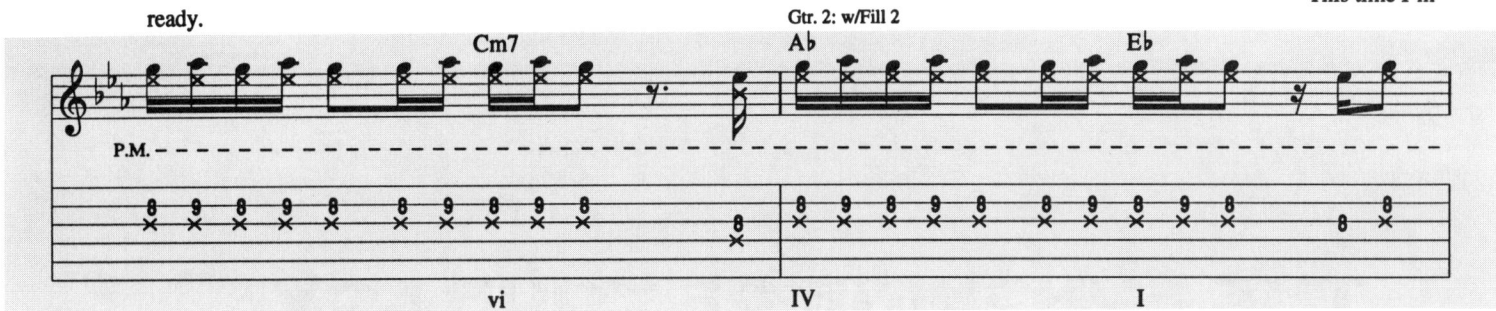
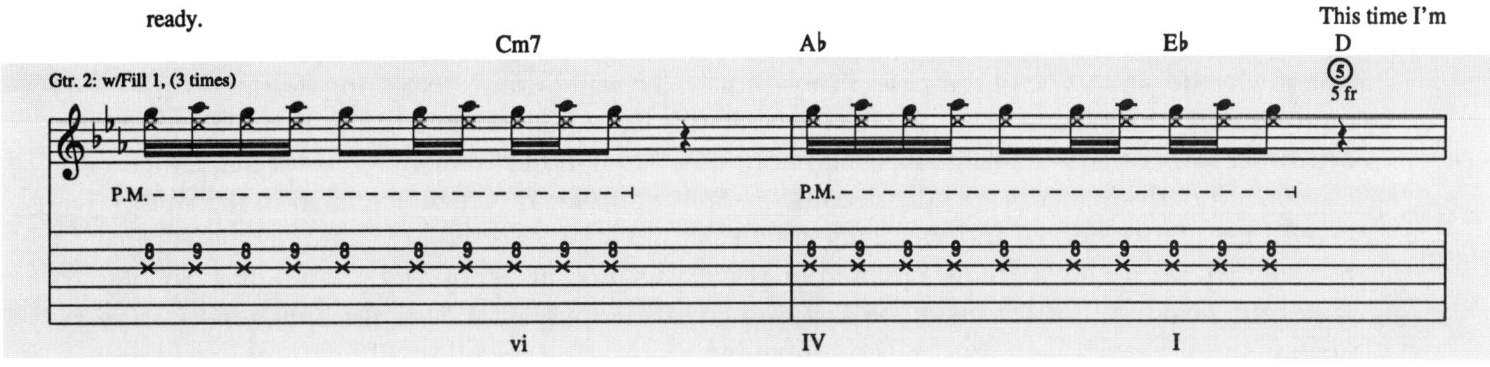

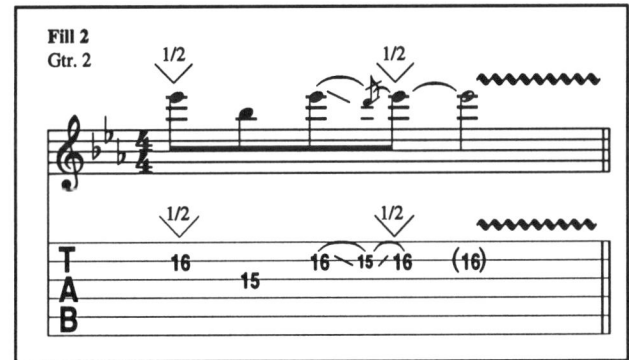
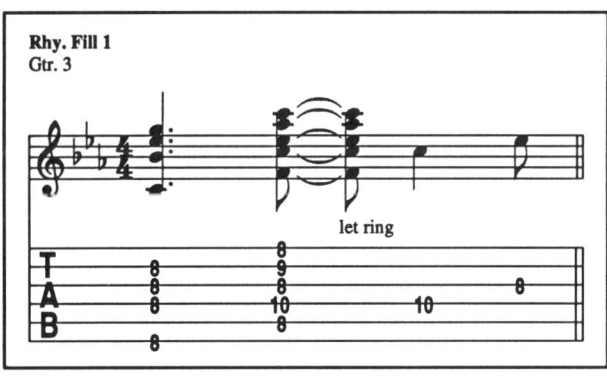
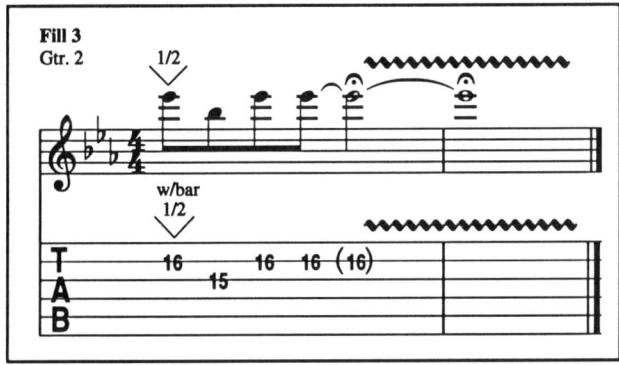
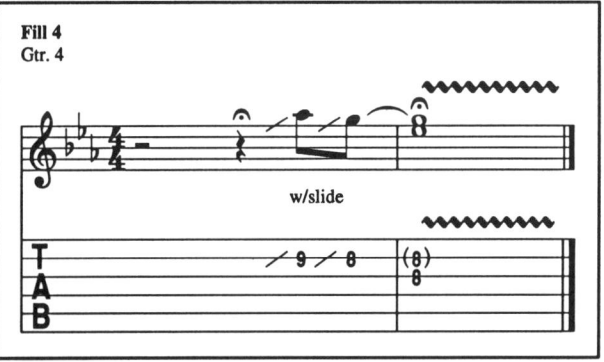

THE SUNSHINE OF YOUR LOVE
Cream

Cream was the prototype of the power trio—guitar, bass and drums exploring loud, improvisatory blues-based rock. Almost two decades later the influence of the Eric Clapton-Jack Bruce-Ginger Baker amalgam is still enormous. Though best remembered for aggressive live concert performances (see "Crossroads" in *Power Studies 1*), Cream excelled in the studio where their compositional and arranging abilities could transcend the physical limitations of the three-piece ensemble. "Sunshine of Your Love" was their first "pop" hit and unquestionably one of the heaviest tunes to make the Top 40 playlists. Reputedly written for Jimi Hendrix, it is a precursor of today's hard rock music containing a powerful, relentless riff, allusions to blues song structure and chord changes (see *Basics 1*) and brilliant guitar work.

The main riff introduced in the opening measures dominates the song—it is heard in the intro [A], verses [B], [D], [G] and behind the solo [F]. During the verses and solo, it incorporates the characteristic I–IV–I moves of the standard 12-bar blues form. (See Movable Riffs in *Basics 2*: Ch. 3.)

Eric's landmark "Sunshine of Your Love" solo is exemplary. He plays with the fire of a rocker and the soul of a bluesman striking that perfect balance which is definitive Clapton. Here his signature use of mixed major and minor pentatonic scales is in full force presenting a textbook case of blues-rock melodic ambiguity. This blend of major and minor sounds and the resulting ambiguity is a mainstay of his style specifically and of blues-rock music in general. (See *Basics 3*: Ch. 3, p. 31). In this D tonal center, the ambiguity would be created through the deliberate use of both major third (F#) and minor third (F) in melody lines (see *Basics 3*: Ch. 7 parallel minor). More on this in *Advanced Concepts and Techniques*.

In the solo's first three bars, the open E form (*Basics 3*: Ch. 4) is used. Eric switches to the open G form (*Basics 3*: Ch. 1) in bars 4-2. These serve to set up a predominately major sound. Over the A–C–G part of the progression, he alternates between minor and major sounds in open E minor form (*Basics 3*: Ch. 1) combined with the open D minor form (*Basics 3*: Ch.4: pp. 40-41)—a time-honored move in blues and rock guitar playing. Check out his string bends of a half-step used consistently in this section to change the quality of the third from minor to major. In the last six bars, Clapton builds to a climax, moving freely between the E minor and D minor forms as well as minor and major combined sounds providing us with an ideal study in combining shapes and mixing minor/major tonality. See both Chapters 6 and 7 in *Basics 3* for more on connecting major and minor forms.

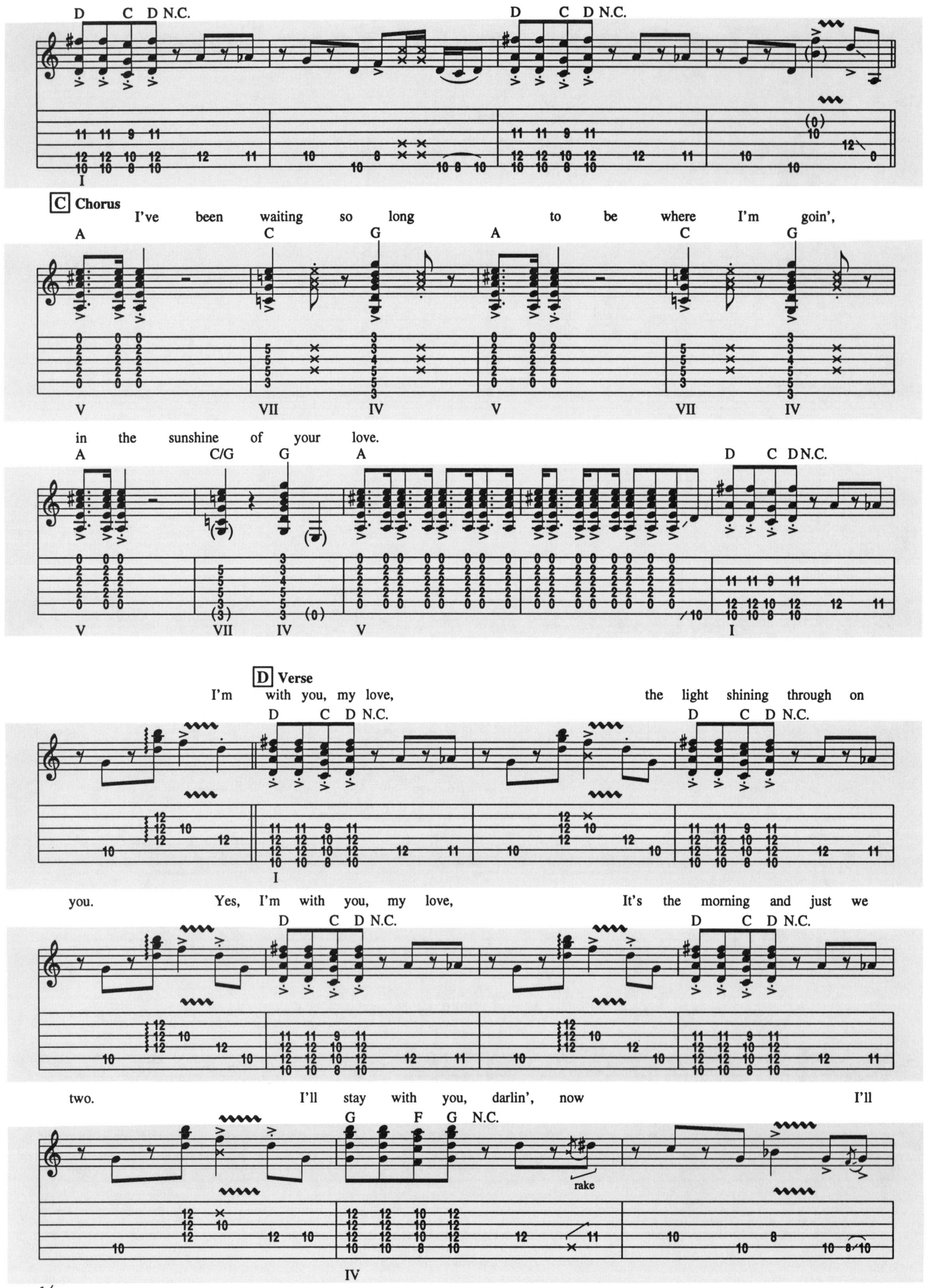

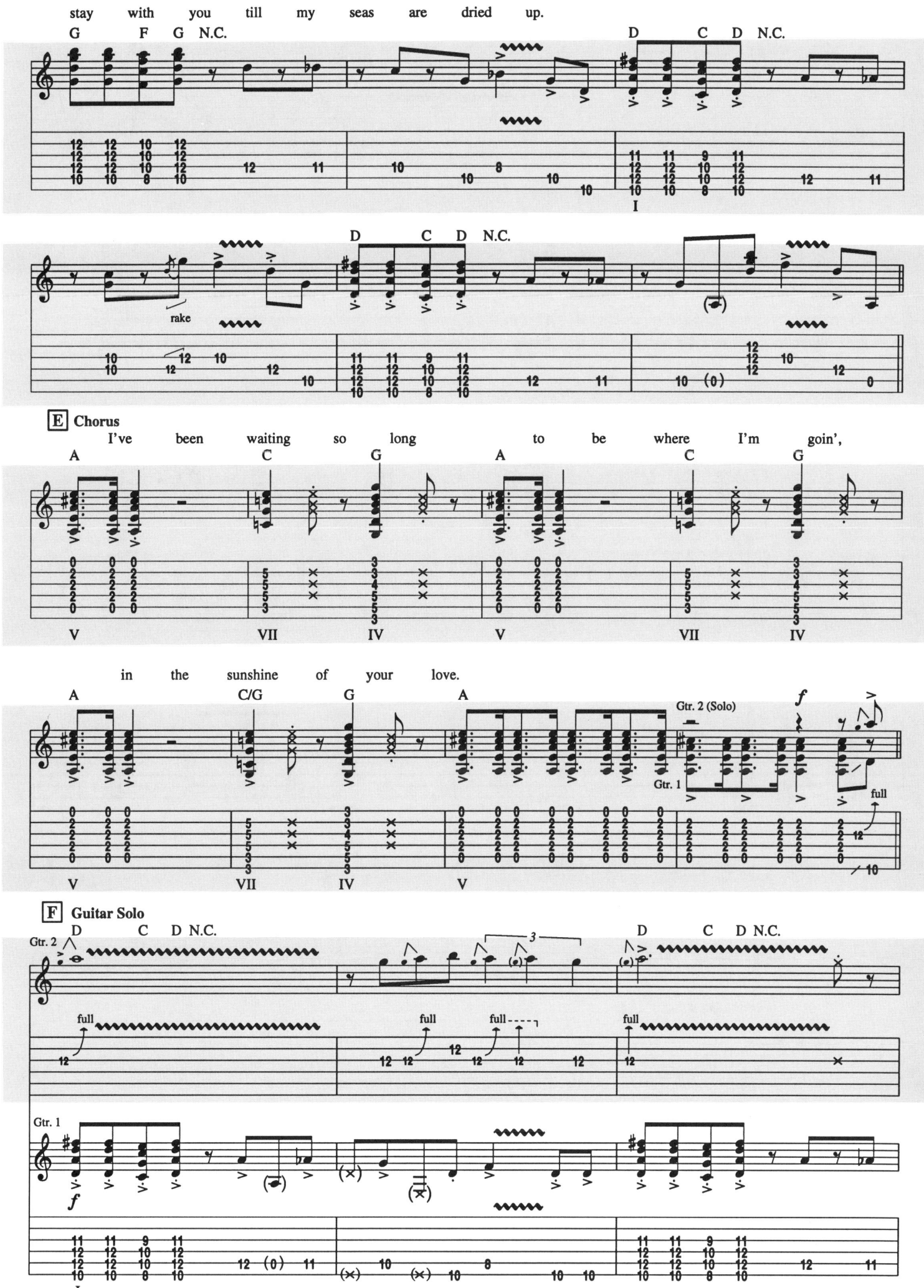

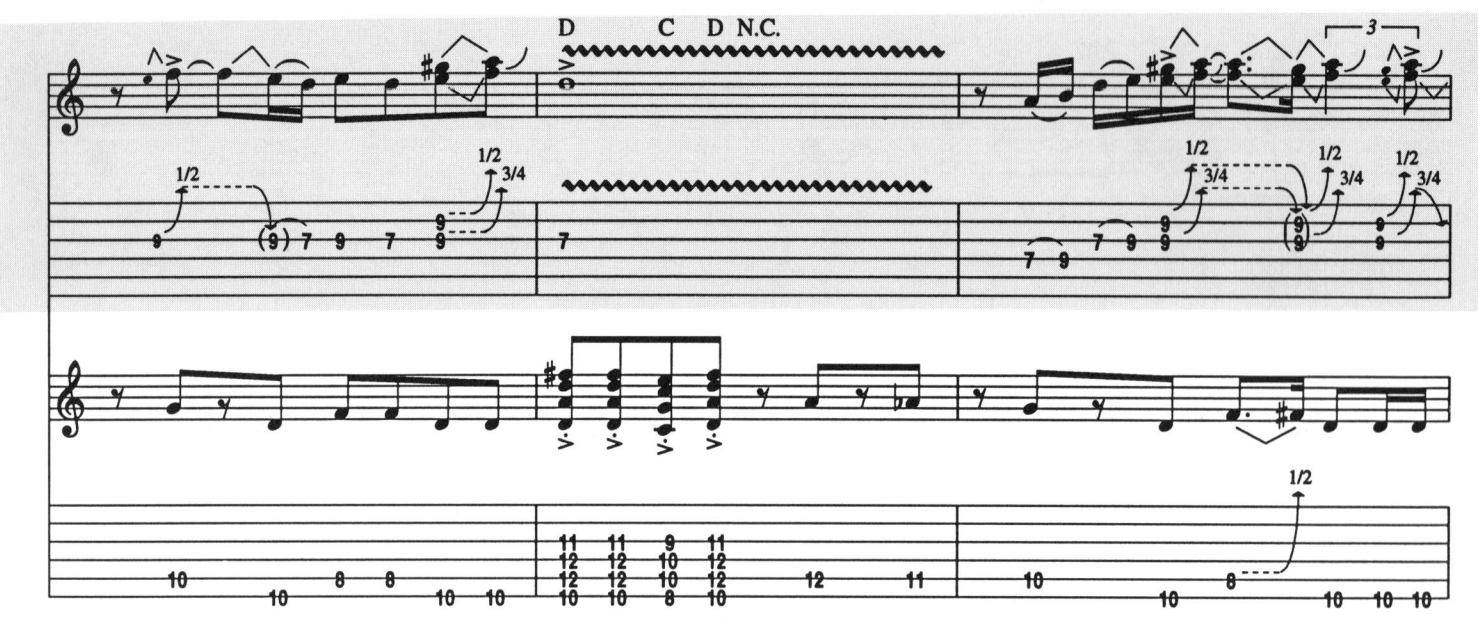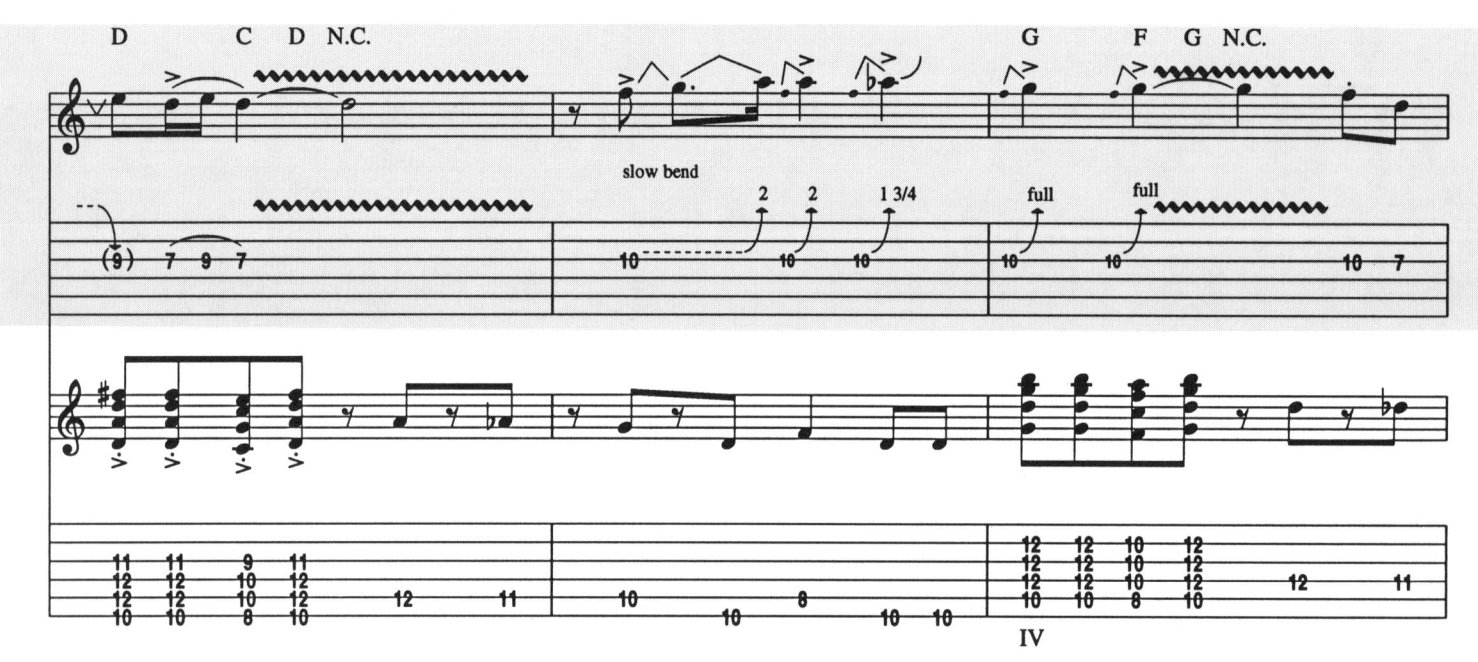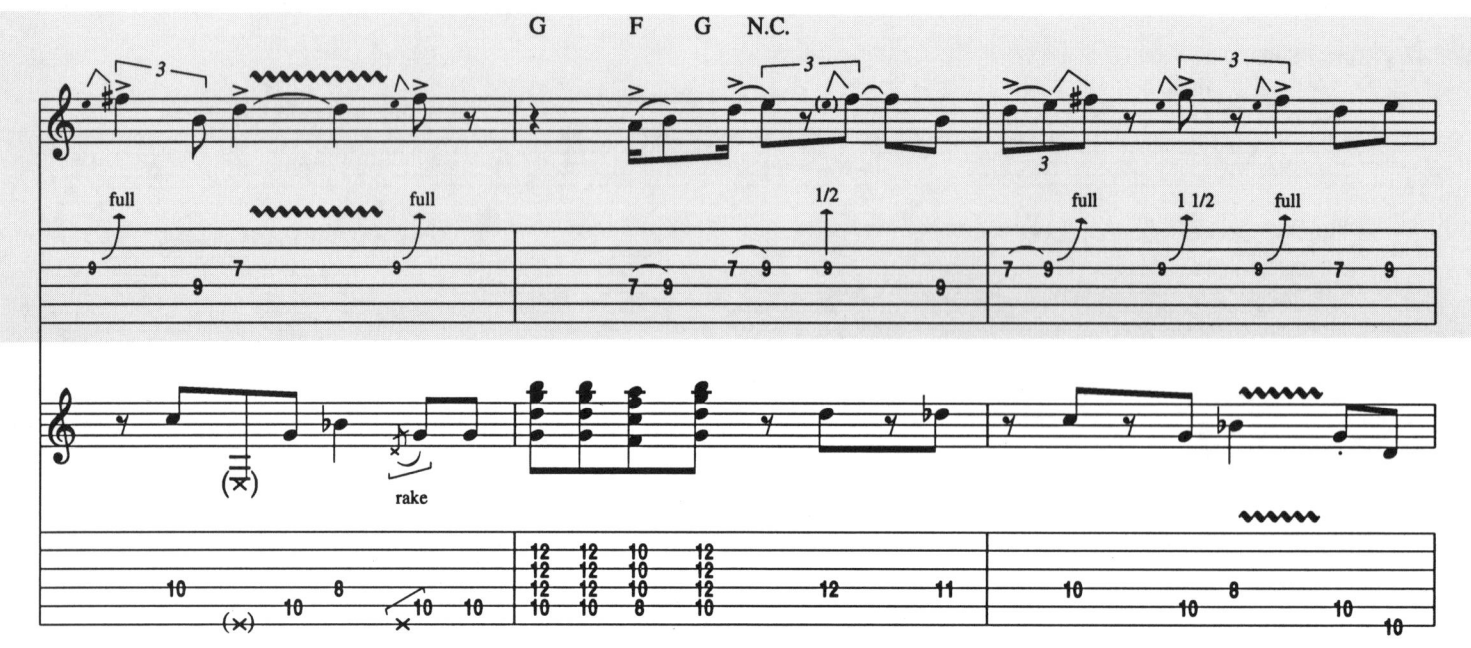

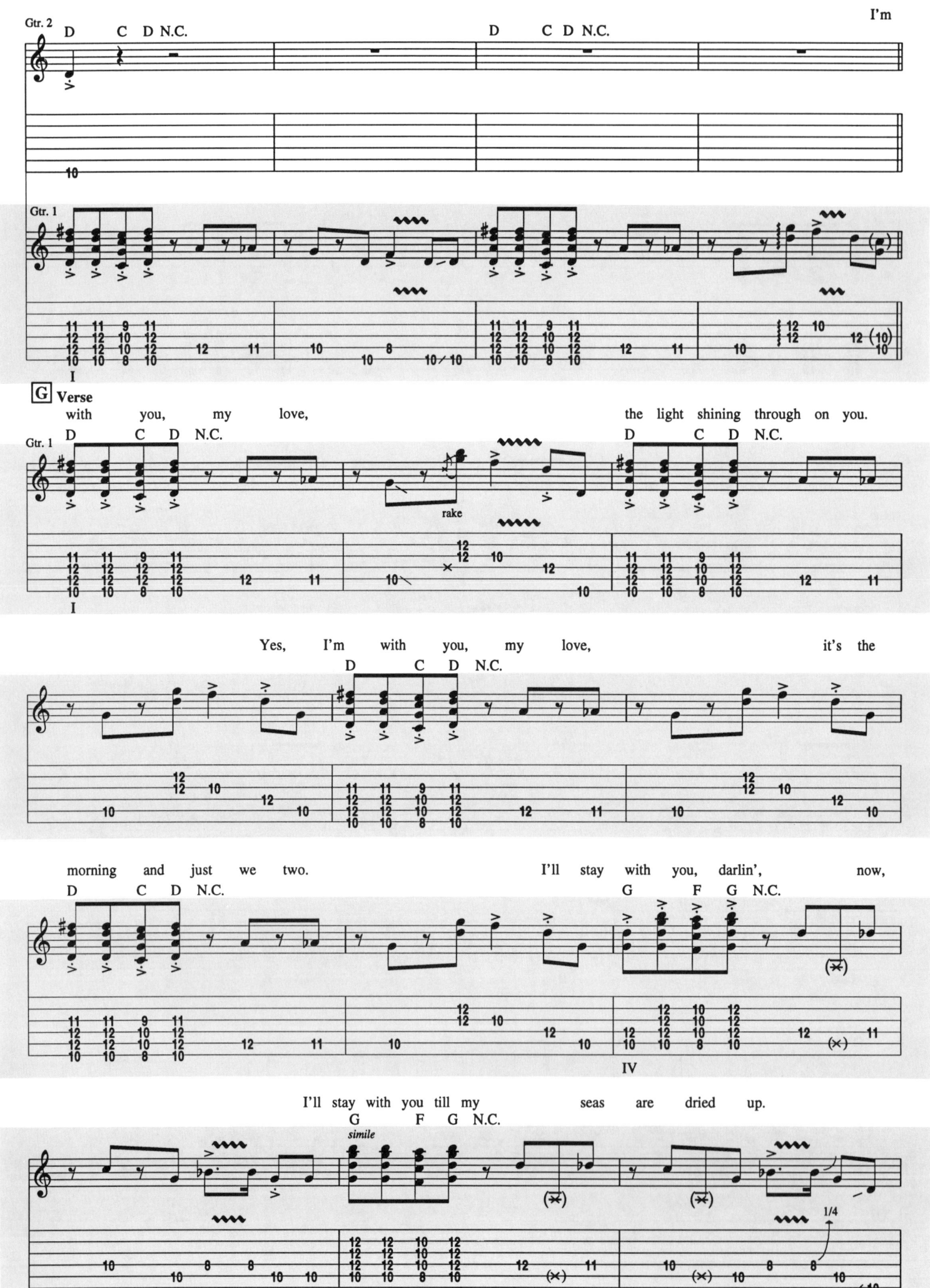

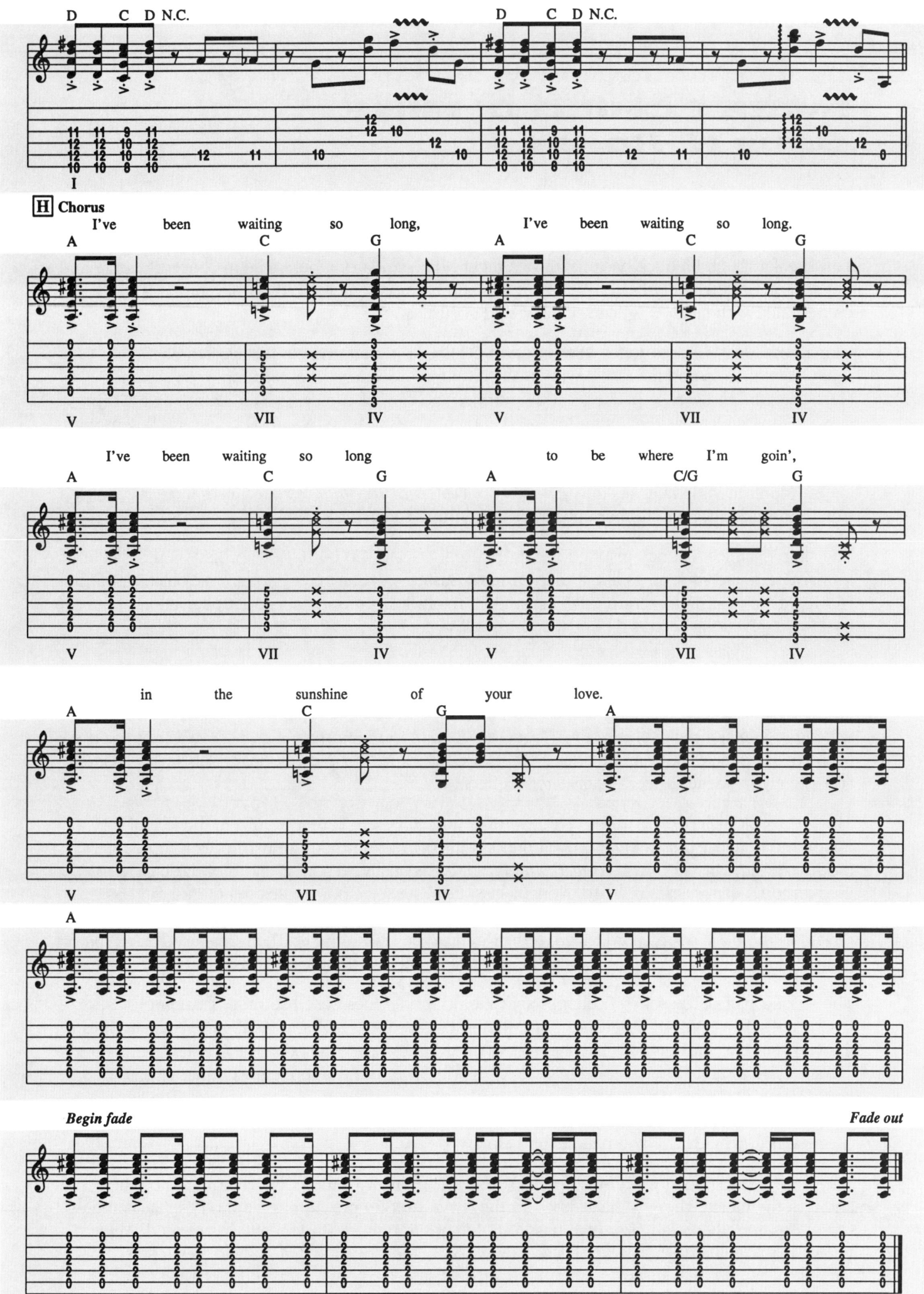

SWEET CHILD O' MINE
Guns N' Roses

The L.A. bad boys truly arrived with their bombastic and trend-setting 1987 debut album, *Appetite for Destruction*. Exuding from every groove on the record is the sound and attitude that announced the birth of a new hard rock music for the '90's. "Sweet Child O' Mine" is a case in point. This breakthrough hit track became an overnight MTV standard, a perennial in-concert favorite and remains one of their very best; full of contrasts and harmonic/melodic/dynamic surprises and well-orchestrated with layers of guitars, electric and acoustic.

Like all of Guns N' Roses' tunes, "Sweet Child O'Mine" is tuned down a half-step to E♭. Get an E♭ note from a piano and then follow the relative tuning procedure in *Basics 1*: p. 6 or use an electronic tuner to get the pitches string by string. You can, of course, use the companion CD or cassette tape which has the tuning recorded and comparison tune by ear. The intro [A] begins with the song's intervallic signature riff–Riff A played by Gtr. 1. This is based on the open D form (*Basics 3*: Ch. 5) and incorporates a wide interval approach to melody with unusual and angular leaps. (More on wide intervals in *Advanced Concepts and Techniques*.) Slash uses a creamy, thick front-humbucker tone to further enhance its distinctive character.

The simple, almost country-inspired verses [B] use a D–C–G–D (I–VII–IV–I) progression indigenous to many standard rock tunes like "Takin' Care of Business," "Can't Get Enough of Your Love" and "All Right Now" in *Power Studies 2*. This section involves layered guitars and arpeggiation of the basic changes in the second 8 bars. (See *Basics 2*: p. 55.)

The chorus [C] beginning on A, the V chord, introduces variations of the opening riff altered to fit the progression of A–C–D (V–VII–I). They are based on the open forms of A form (*Basics 3*: Ch. 3) and D form. During the ending of the verse, Slash gets in some tasty, country-flavored melodic soloing in D major pentatonic derived from the open G form (*Basics 3*: Ch. 1). You'll hear the use of the major pentatonic with the added 4th, G. Jeff Beck in "People Get Ready" also uses this tone consistently to creates a melodically similar effect.

The guitar solo [D] involves a key change and a mode change. This section is in the key of E minor and here Slash uses the E natural minor scale or Aeolian mode primarily. (For more on modes see *Advanced Concepts and Techniques*.) Occasionally, on the B chord of the progression, the harmonic minor Scale is heard. Nonetheless, these new diatonic scales still fit into our basic framework of minor melody/chord forms as covered in *Basics 3* and it's as easy to visualize them related to the basic open chord forms as their pentatonic counterparts. The forms used are E minor form (*Basics 3*: Ch. 1), A minor form (*Basics 3*: Ch. 2) and D minor form (*Basics 3*: Ch. 4).

The second part of the solo [E] changes character to more blues-based sounds. Slash improvises over a I–III–IV–VI–VII–III progression in E minor: Em–G–A–C–D–G and it's E minor pentatonic all the way. He positions his licks largely in the typical "blues box" E minor form (*Basics 2*: Ch. 4 and *Basics 3*: Ch. 1) and D minor form (*Basics 3*: Ch. 4). Check out the sequence (*Basics 3*: p. 9) in bars 11 and 12. This is an ascending pattern with repeated notes in its pattern units. The fast ostinato riffs which follow should present no problems once you work them out technically. (Review *Basics 2*: Ch. 4 if you need extra help.)

The outro [F] incorporates wah-wah pedal sounds. The throw of the pedal is indicated by the + and o in the music. The + is the symbol for the down (treble) position and the o designates the up (bass) position. By rocking from the bass to treble position the wah-wah effect is created. After you've mastered the technique in this section go back and learn the wah solo in Stevie Ray Vaughan's "Scratch-n-sniff" in *Power Studies 1* for some very useful extra study. The lead lines again use open E minor and D minor forms of the E minor pentatonic scale.

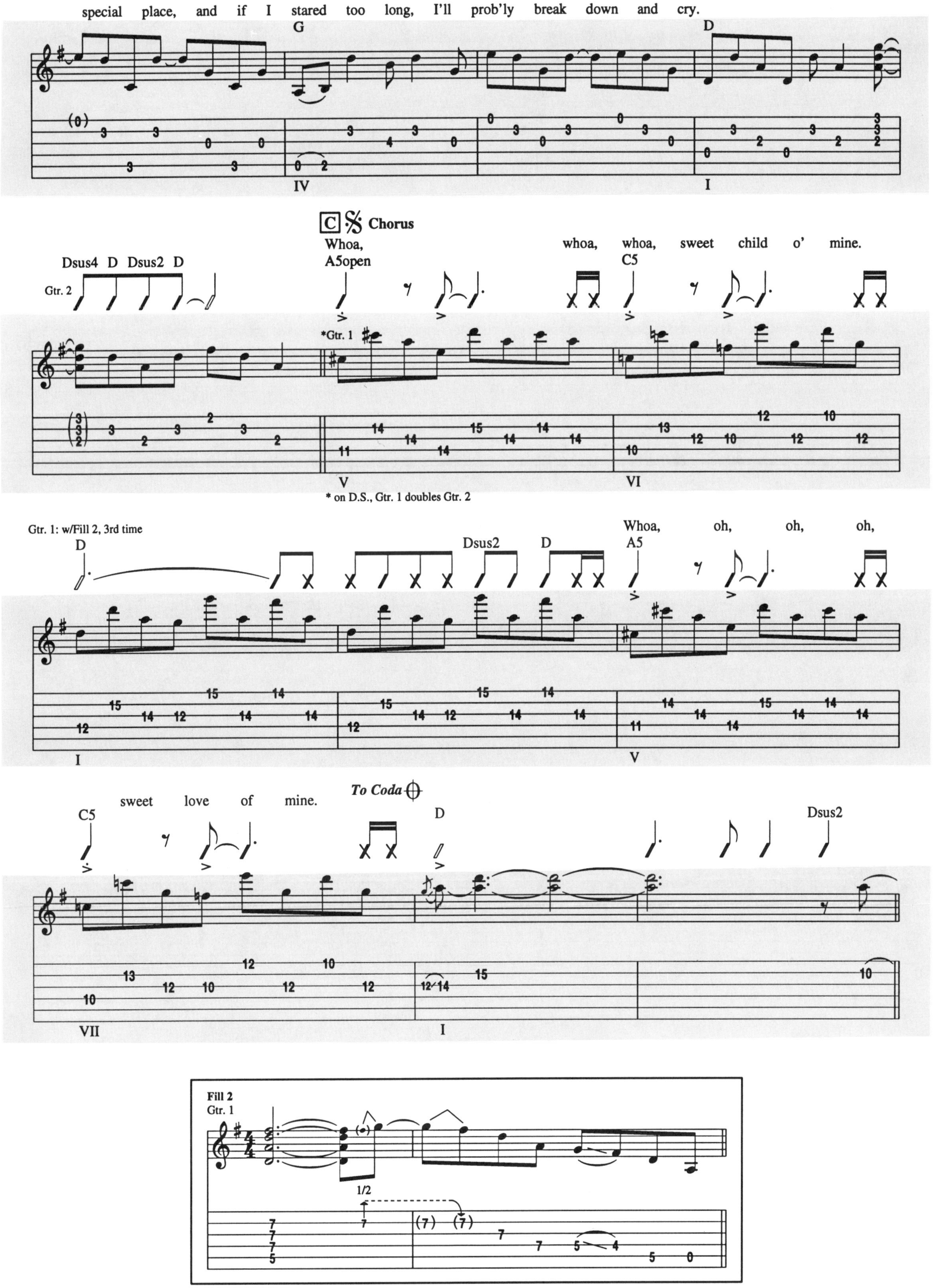
special place, and if I stared too long, I'll prob'ly break down and cry.
G
D
IV
I
C
Chorus
Whoa, whoa, whoa, sweet child o' mine.
A5open
C5
Dsus4 D Dsus2 D
Gr. 2
*Gtr. 1
V
VI
* on D.S., Gtr. 1 doubles Gtr. 2
Gtr. 1: w/Fill 2, 3rd time
D
Dsus2
D
Whoa, oh, oh, oh,
A5
I
V
sweet love of mine.
C5
To Coda
D
Dsus2
VII
I
Fill 2
Gtr. 1
1/2

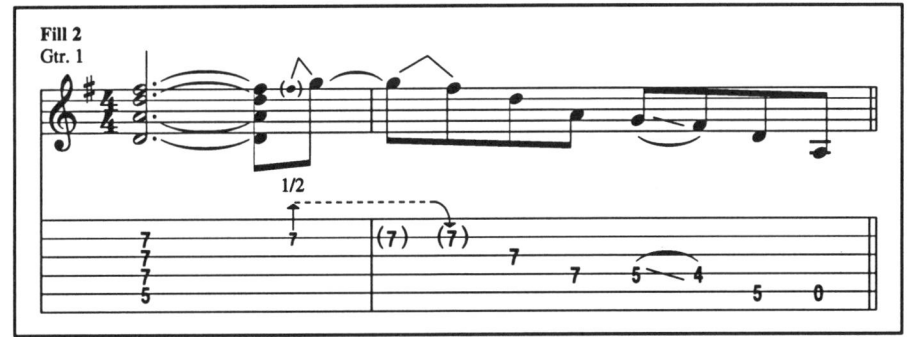

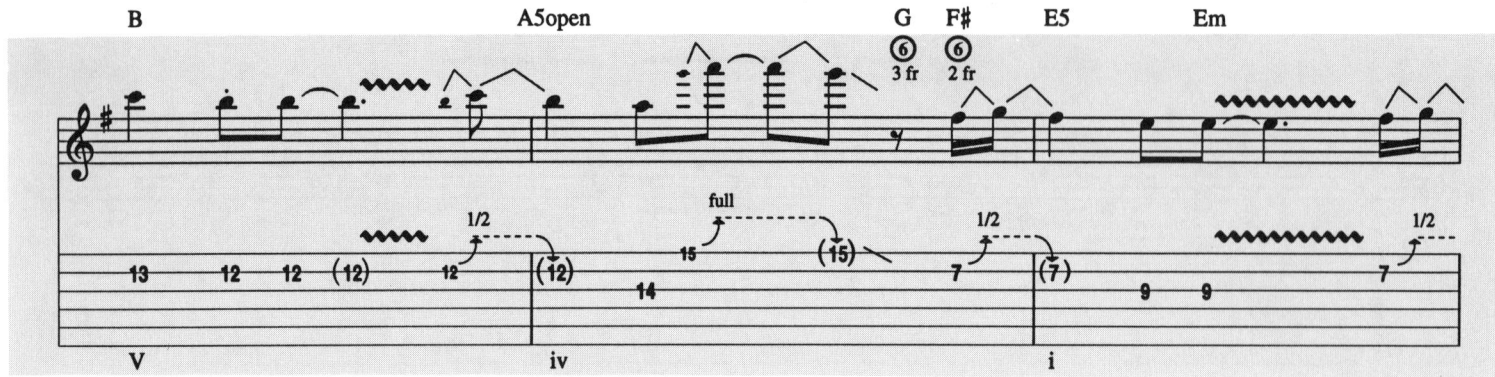
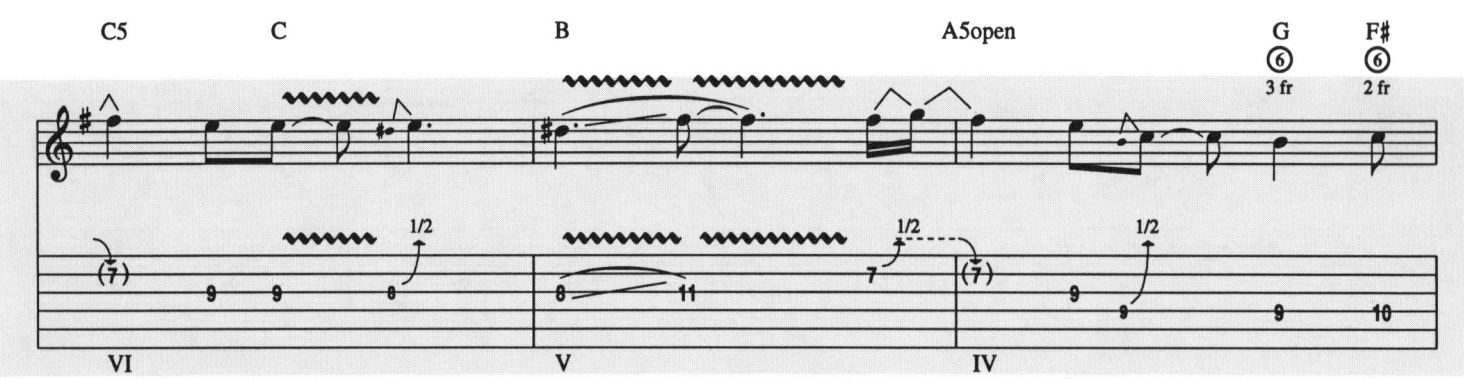
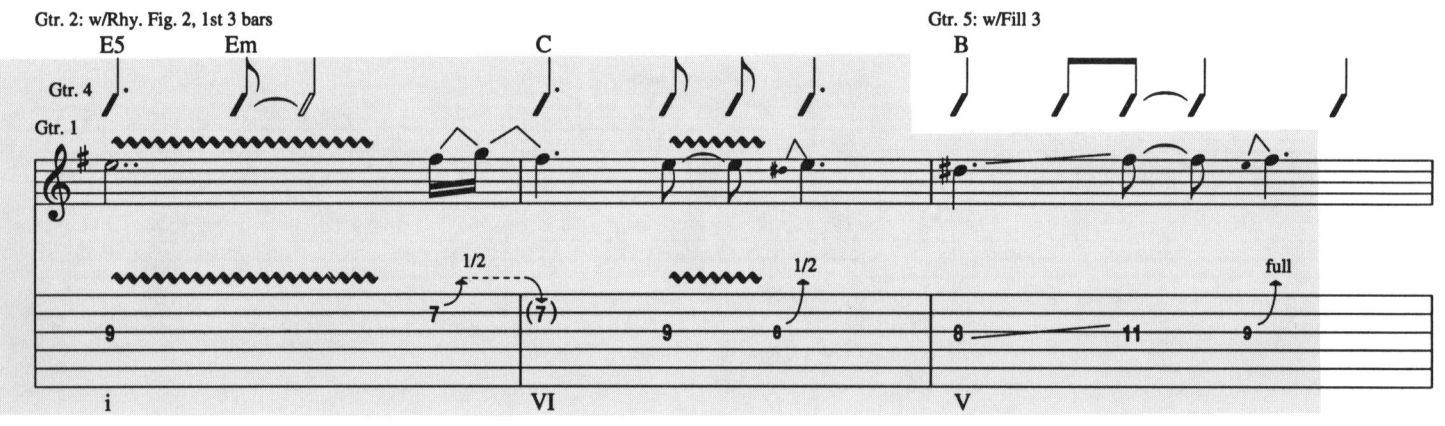
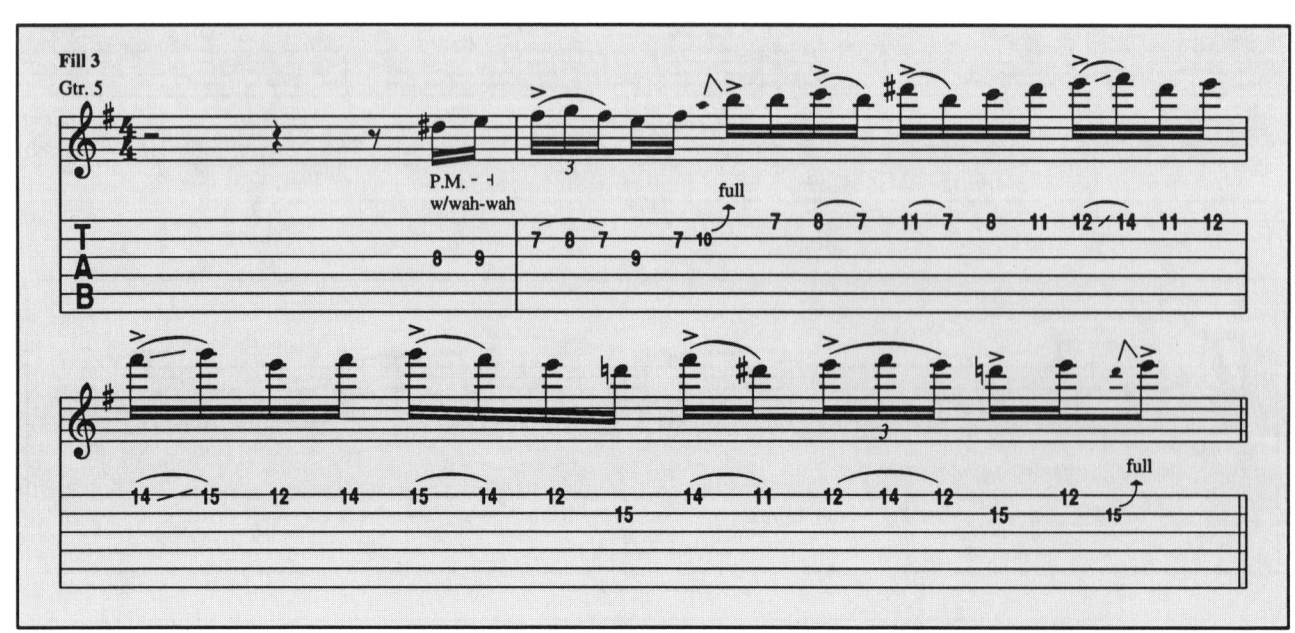

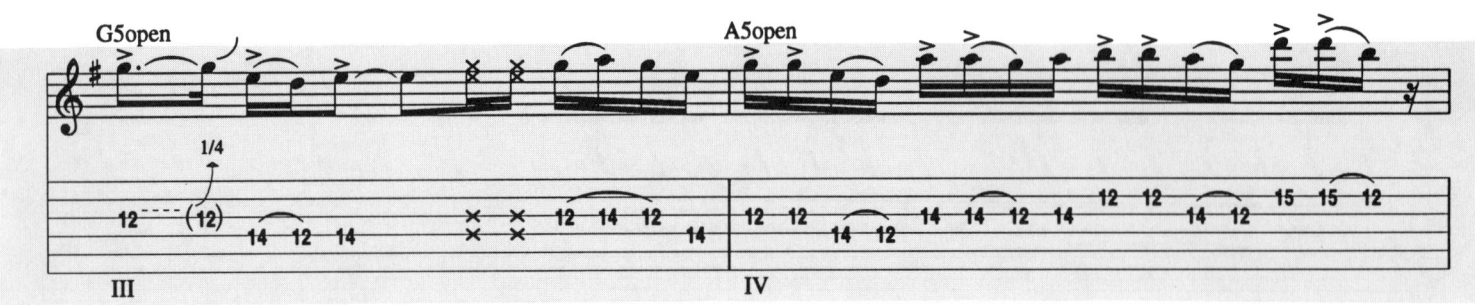
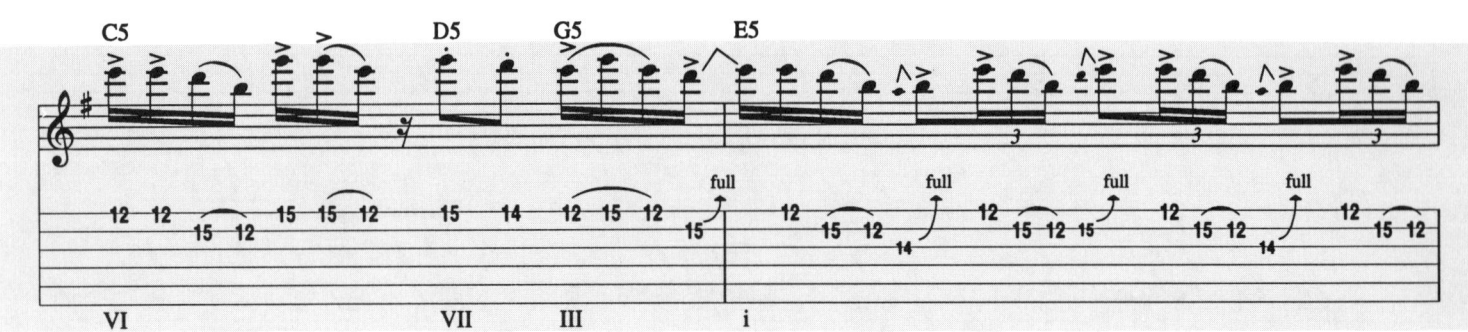
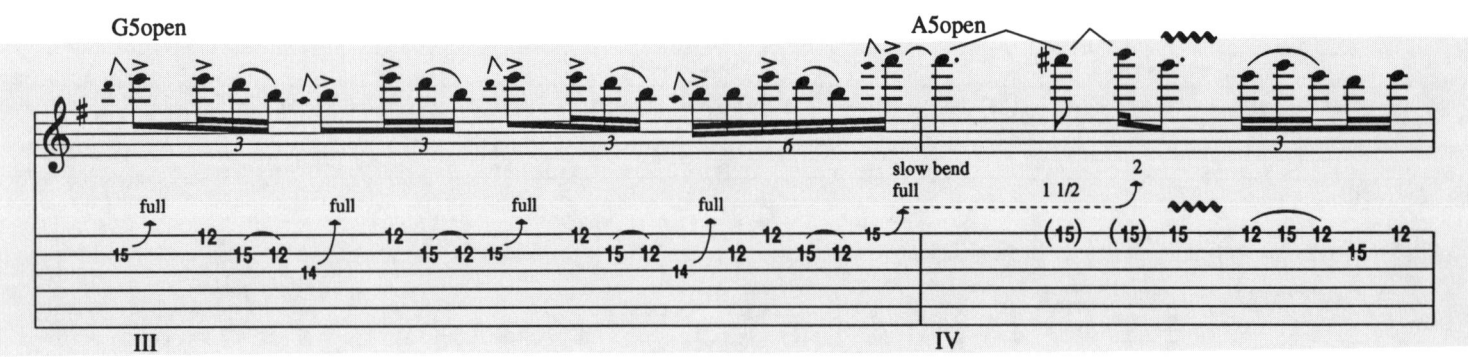
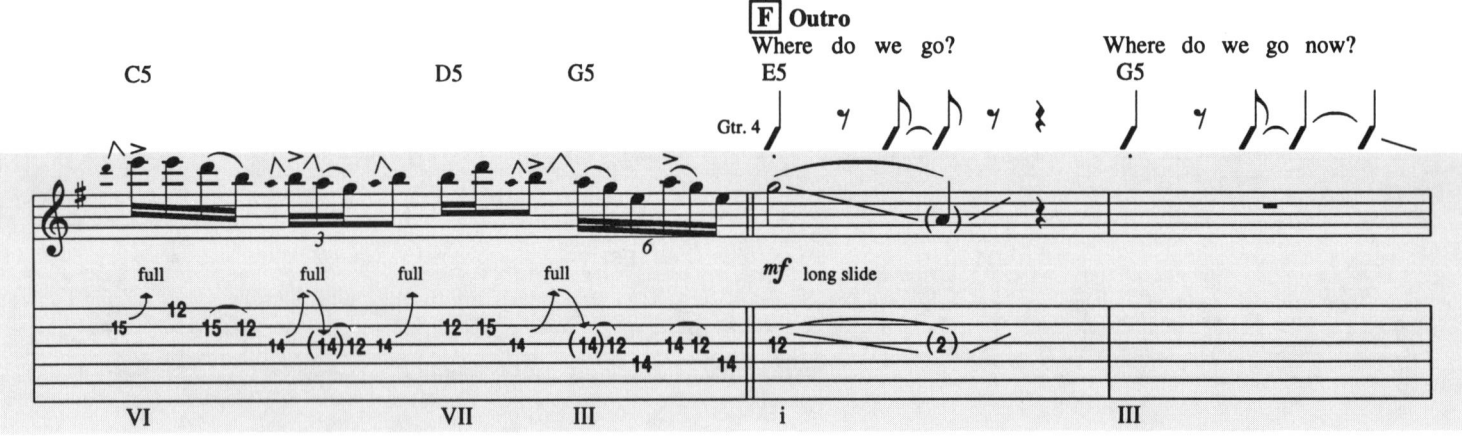
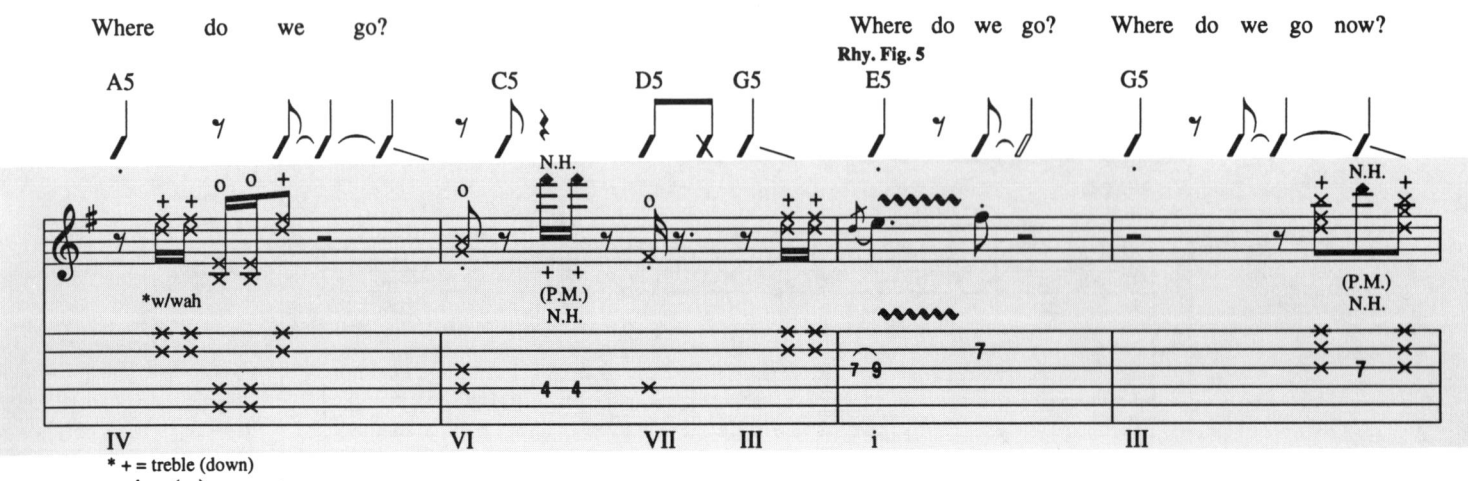

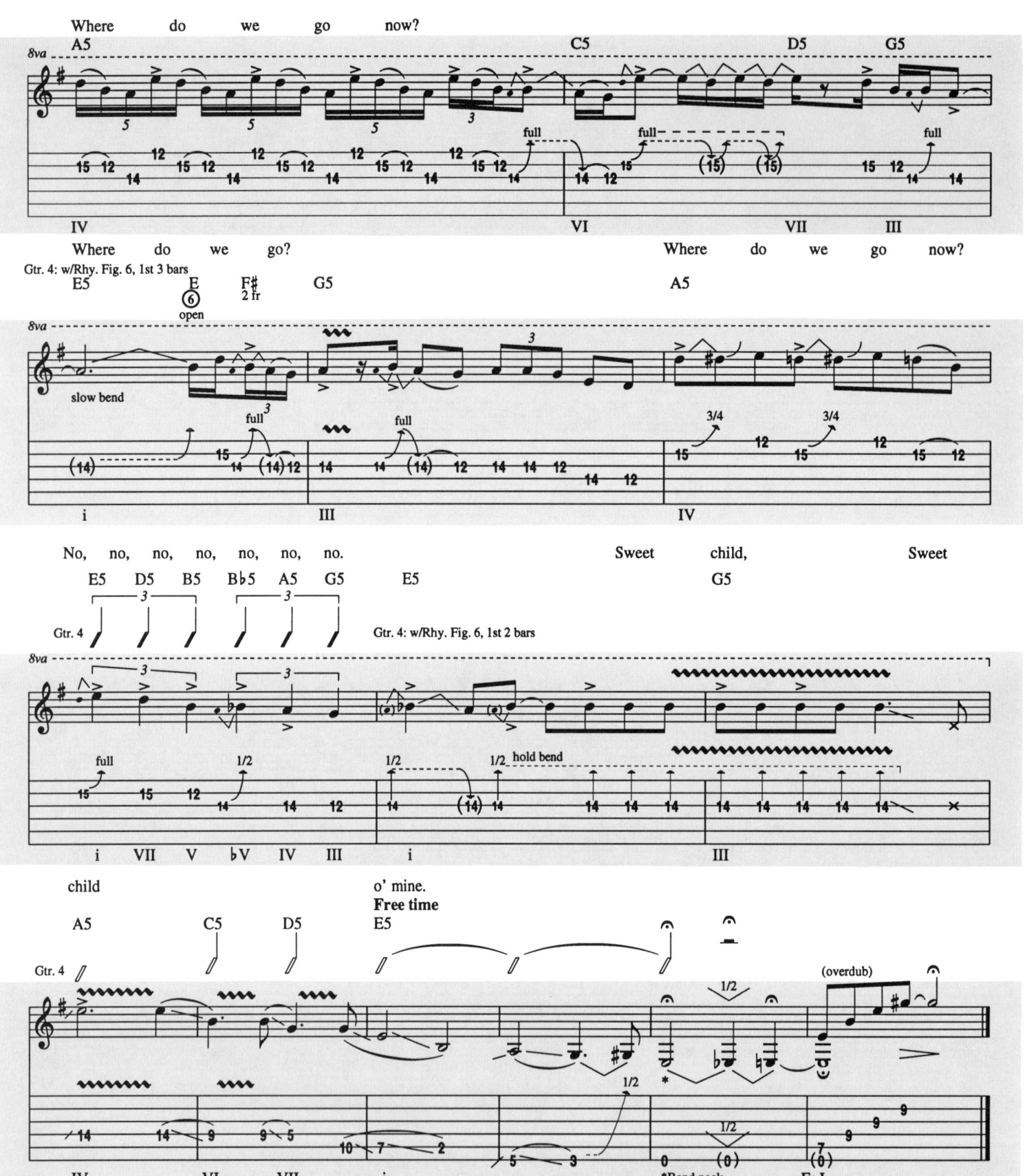

Additional Lyrics

She's got eyes of the bluest skies,
as if they thought of rain.
I hate to look into those eyes
and see an ounce of pain.
Her hair reminds me of a warm safe place
where as a child I'd hide.
And pray for the thunder and the rain
to quietly pass me by.

(To Chorus:)

LENNY
Stevie Ray Vaughan

This moody and atmospheric ballad from Stevie Ray Vaughan's 1984 debut album *Texas Flood* presents the leading bluesman of the 1980's in a dramatically different context. Considered to be one of his career pinnacles and a musical milestone in the genre, "Lenny" embodies many of the blues and rock influences of which Stevie was so proud. Like all of Stevie's music, "Lenny" is tuned down a half-step to E flat. (See "Sweet Child O' Mine" for a reference to E♭ tuning.)

The intro [A], head [B], head restatement [D] and outro [F] make use of the attractive chord-melody style indigenous to R&B and soul music a la Curtis Mayfield, Jimi Hendrix et al. Stevie employs just a handful of chords and well-placed fills to make a simple but beautiful main theme—in jazz and blues parlance, the "head". Check out the fingered shape used for the IV chord, A6 (bar 6). This shape is moved around the fretboard to produce a B6–D6–G6–B♭6 progression. Note both the typical hammer-on/pull-off (*Basics 3*: p. 15) approach to filling melody and the consistent use of the vibrato bar to bend chords and individual tones.

The solos and fills provide a valuable study in combining pentatonic forms in the key center of E. Make sure you assign each melody line to its corresponding open chord form to gain a solid understanding of the fretboard chord/scale geography. The solos take place over a repeating I–IV (E to A) progression. With no background chords to specify the exact type of chord—major, minor or dominant–Stevie takes great liberties in his improvisation to deliver colorful and contrasting melodies. The first phrases of Solo 1 [C] are clearly major pentatonic and slide up the neck connecting open A, G, E and D major forms (*Basics 3*: Ch. 6) much in the vein of Jimi's playing in "May This Be Love". The next section is a contrasting parallel minor lick (*Basics 3*: Ch. 7) in open E minor form. Here Stevie uses an Albert Collins-style double-stop approach and fingerpicking (*Basics 2*: Ch. 5). An alternation between parallel minor and major sounds continues through the solo's course essentially in and around the 12th position E minor or E major form (*Basics 3*: Chapters 1 and 4).

In Solo 2 [E], Stevie again begins in the major mode with a strong line in the open G form (*Basics 3*: Ch. 1). A number of forms are used in the first 8 bars open A form (*Basics 3*: Ch. 3), open E form (*Basics 3*: Ch. 4) and open D form (*Basics 3*: Ch. 5). Check out the R&B/country-inspired double-stops and chord-melody licks in bars 5-7. Parallel minor ideas dominate the rest of the solo. Stevie plays this section with a variety of approaches. Highlights include the delta-based open position ostinato riffs in E minor pentatonic (*Basics 1*: p. 56), the Albert King-flavored string bends in the open D minor form (*Basics 3*: Ch. 4) and the high-energy minor pentatonic sequence as the solo's climax. The cadenza [G] is played in free time and recalls and elaborates on the intro's mood. Check out the textbook major pentatonic run that begins the section. Here Stevie strings together the G, E and A forms.

For those of you out there who can't, as I can't, get enough of Stevie Ray Vaughan, the video concert *Live at the Mocambo* is highly recommended. Though unassuming in its production values, it captures the spirit and atmosphere of his nightclub performance in the early days—around the time that *Texas Flood* was recorded. The first encore number was "Lenny" that night and is well worth viewing as an adjunct to this power study.

From the Epic recording TEXAS FLOOD

Lenny

By Stevie Ray Vaughan

Tune Down 1/2 Step
① = Eb   ④ = Db
② = Bb   ⑤ = Ab
③ = Gb   ⑥ = Eb

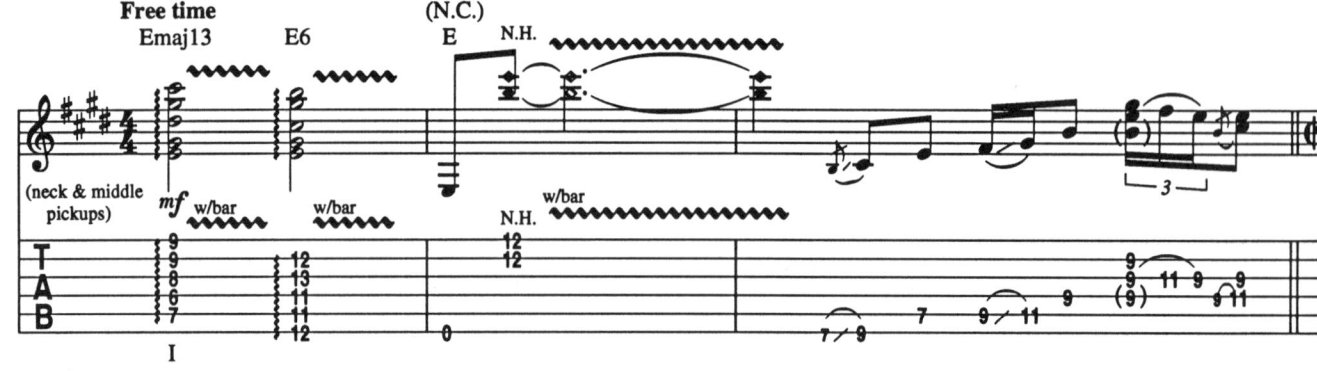

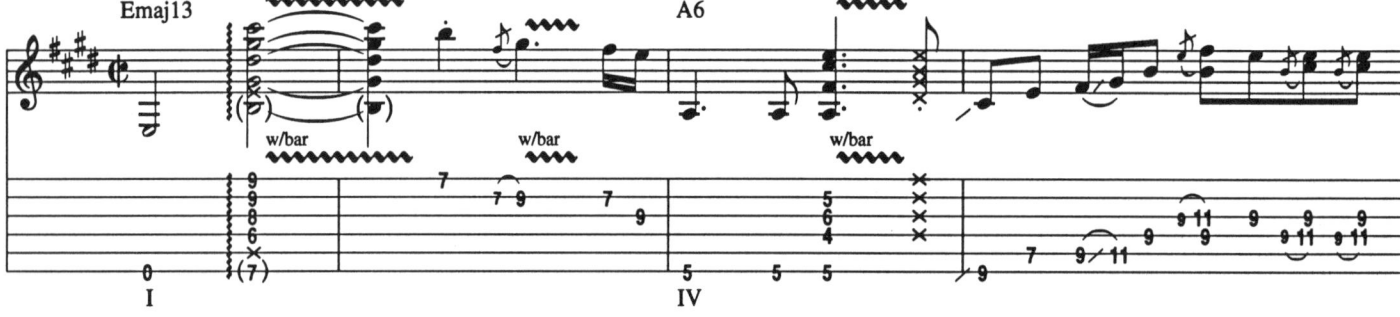

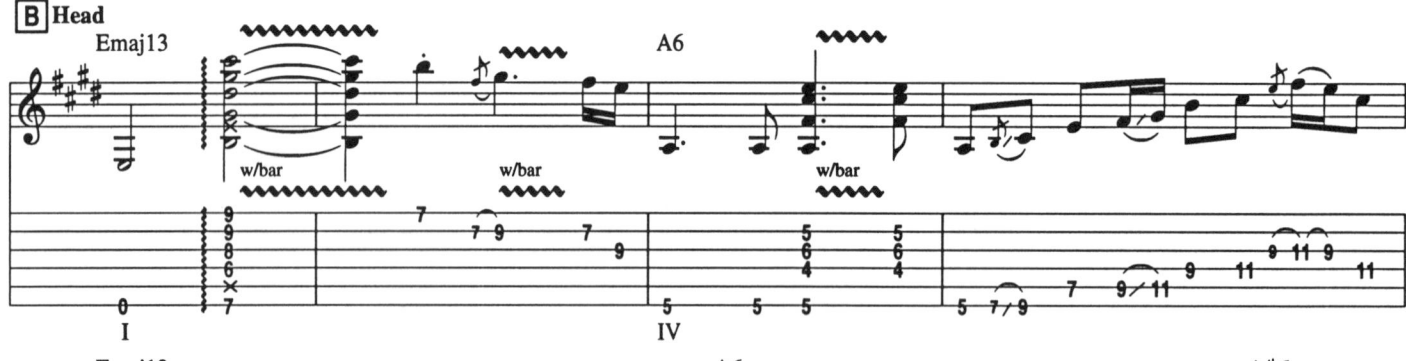

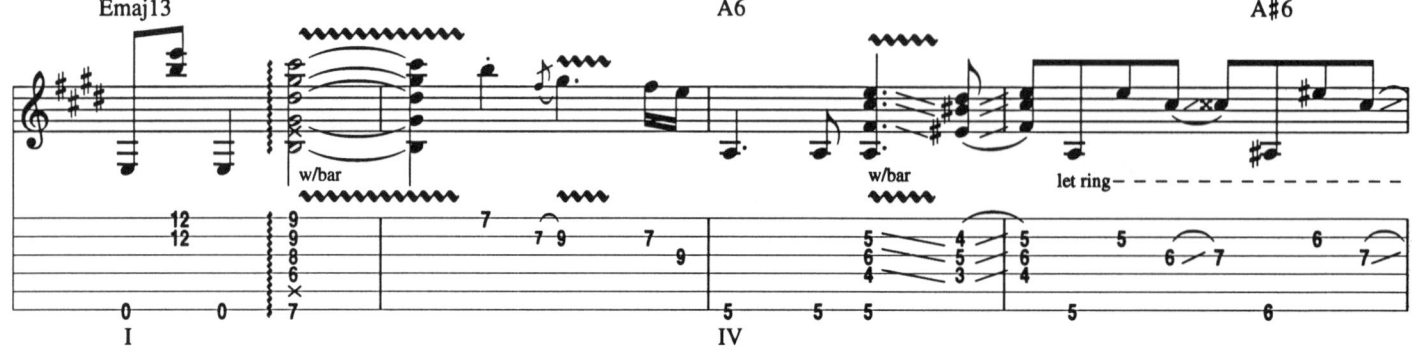

Copyright © 1980 by RAY VAUGHAN MUSIC, INC.
International Copyright Secured   All Rights Reserved

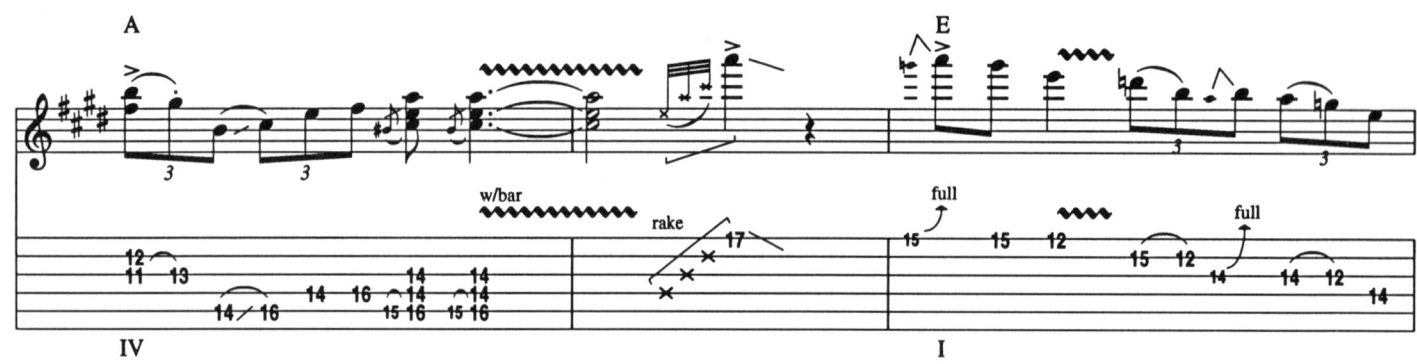
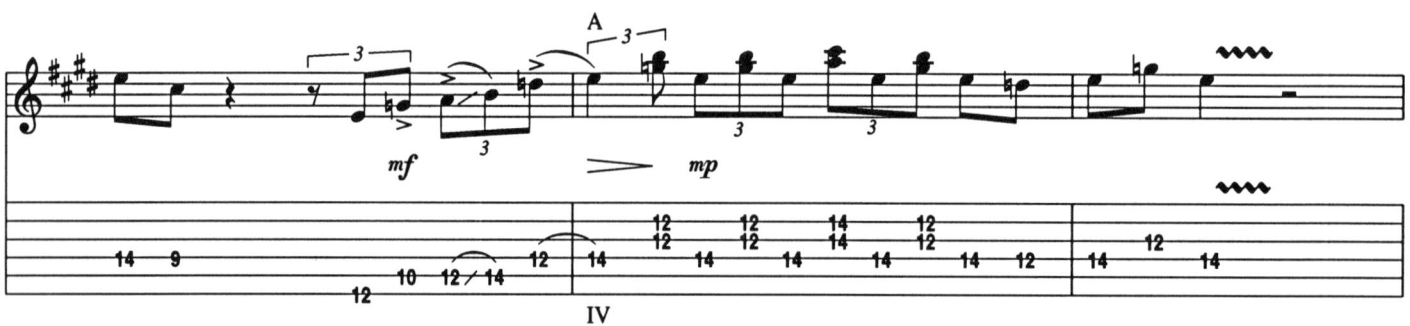
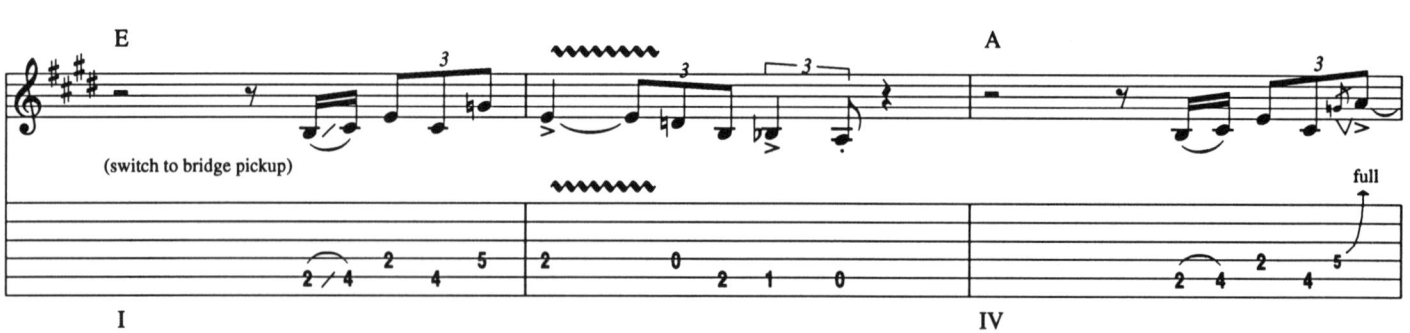
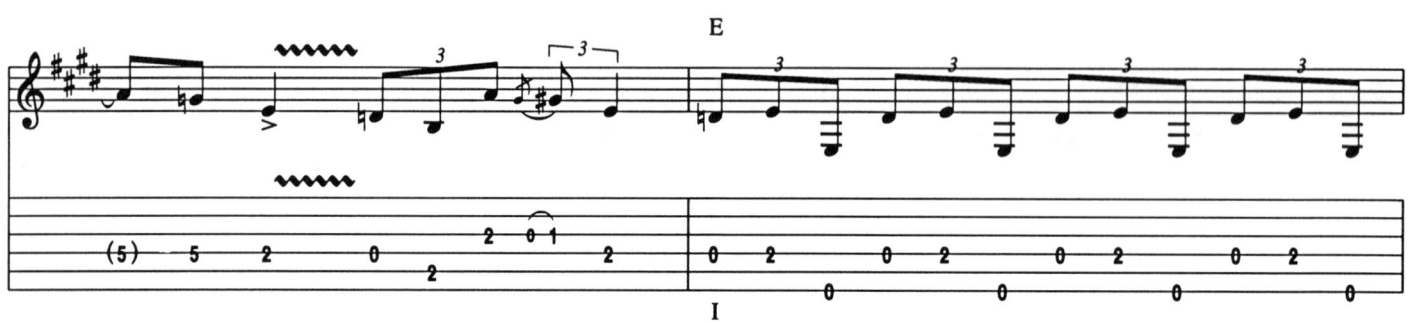

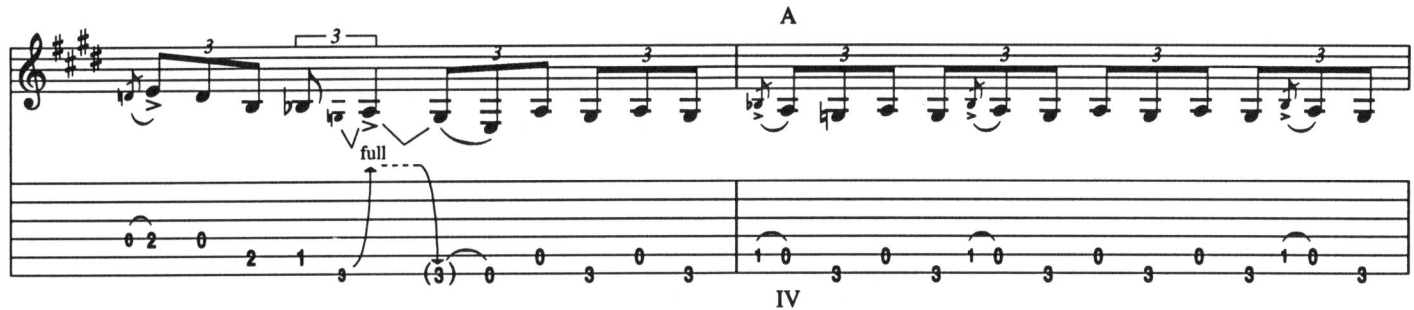

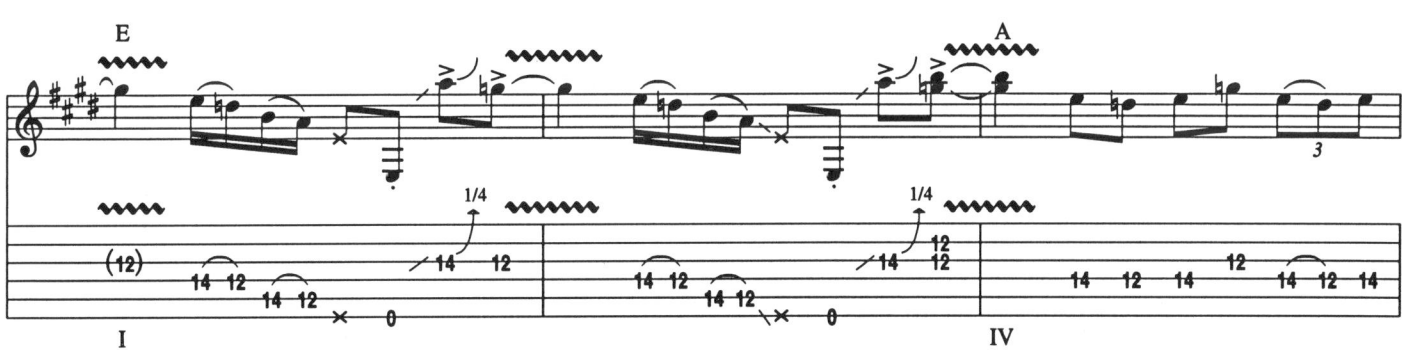
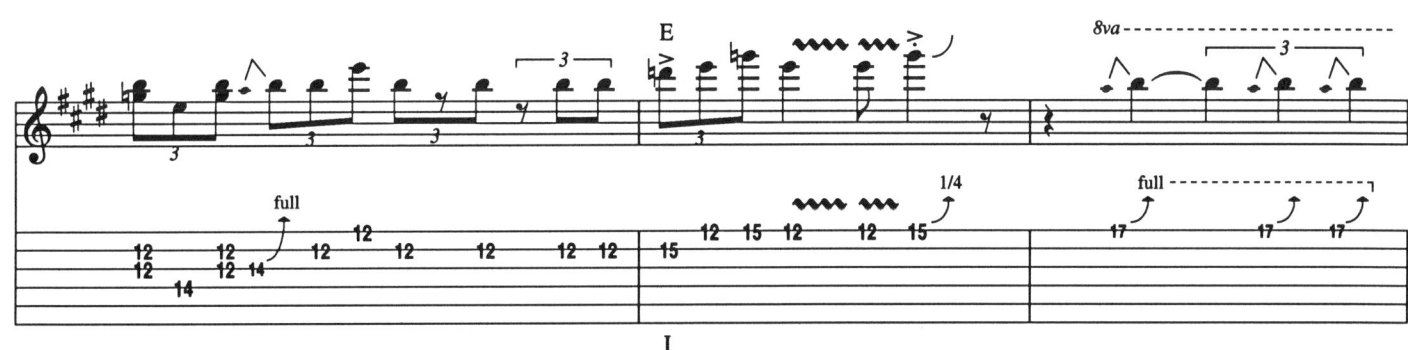

37

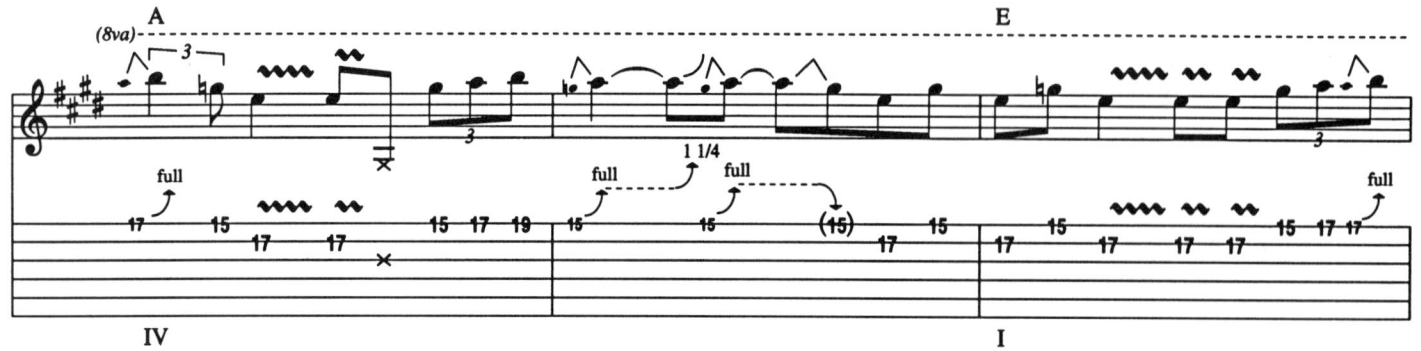
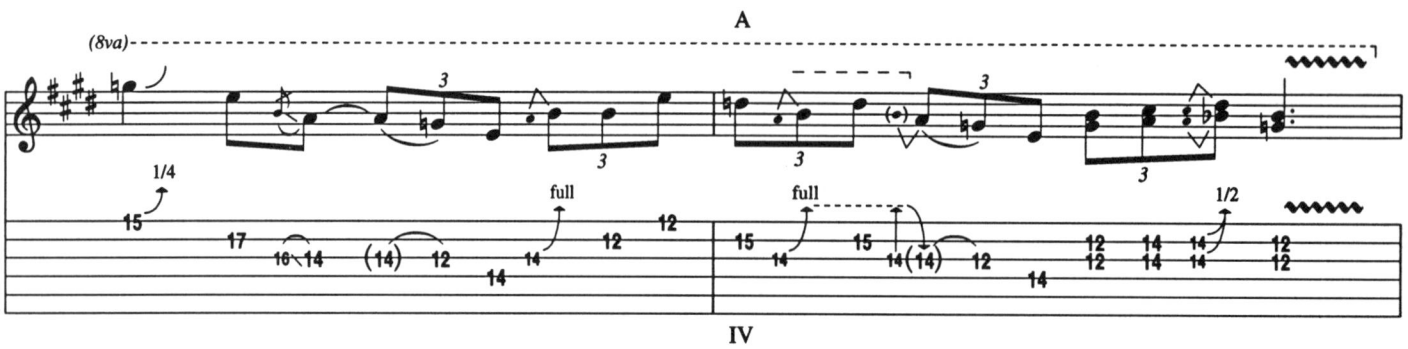
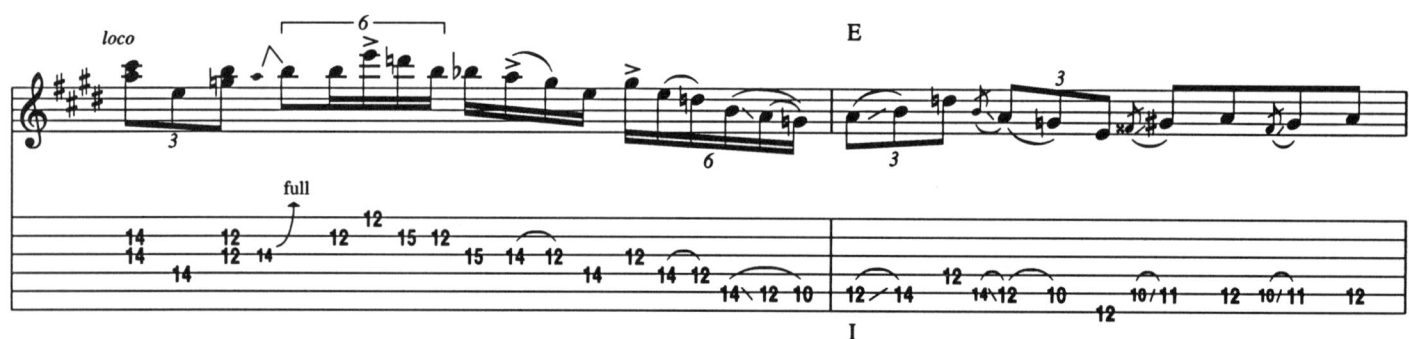
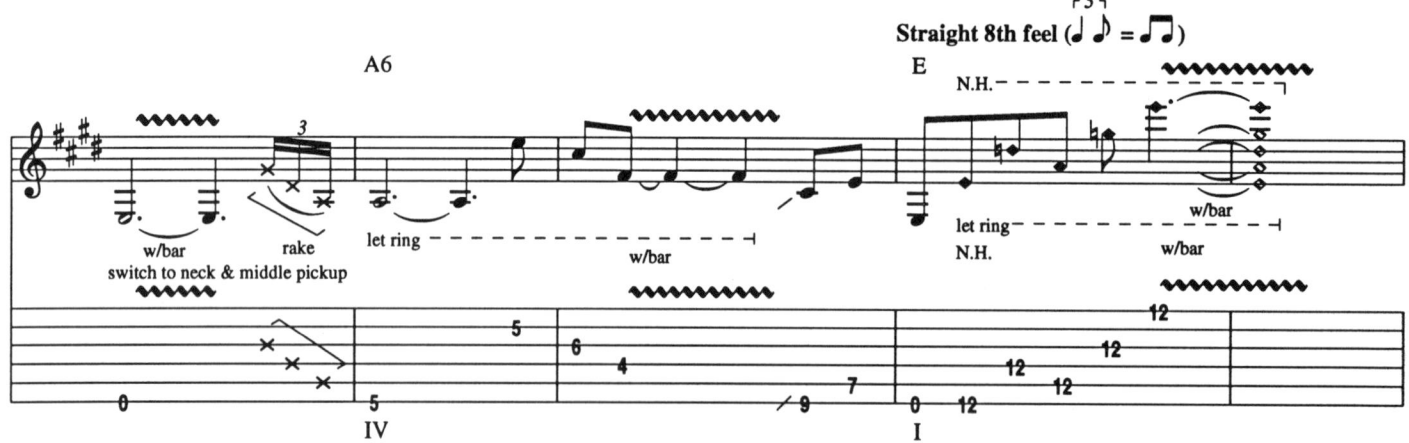
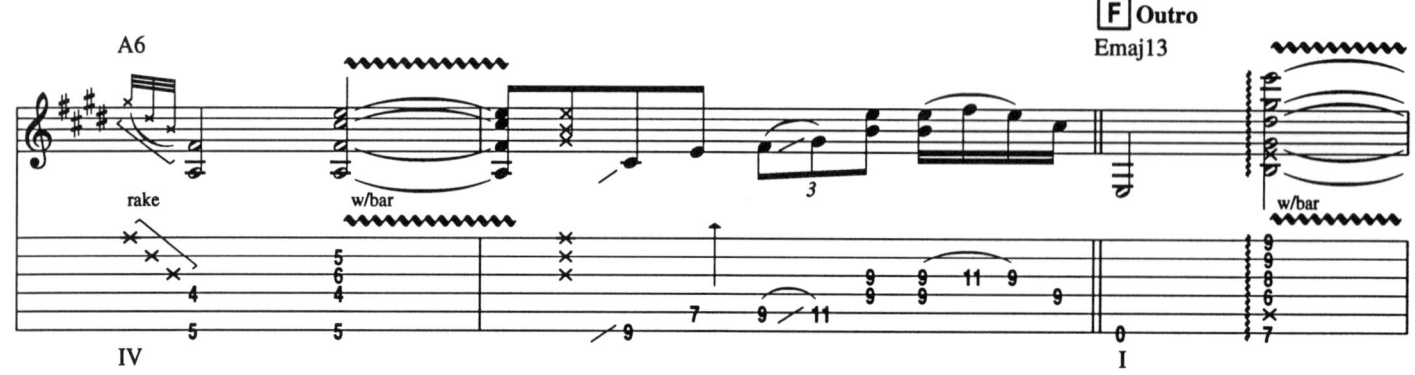

HIDEAWAY
Blues Breakers – John Mayall with Eric Clapton

Eric Clapton's cover of "Hideaway" was so influential it began a tradition that endured through the early history of British blues in the first three Blues Breakers bands. His formula? A supercharged reinterpretation of (Texas/Chicago bluesman) Freddy King's hit instrumental. Clapton's "Hideaway" in 1966 led to successor Peter Green's 1967 version of "The Stumble" which led in turn to "Driving Sideways" a vehicle for Mick Taylor (who later joined the Stones).

"Hideaway" is a 12-bar shuffle-feel blues in E (see *Basics 1* and *Basics 2*) with numerous internal contrasts–varied riffs, melodic hooks, improvised solos and feel changes. The head or main theme is a catchy melody in major pentatonic. This is played in G form (*Basics 3*: Ch. 1) and open E form (*Basics 3*: Ch. 4). As preparation, review the open E blues progressions in *Basics 2*: Ch. 6 and the blues melody pieces at the end of the first five chapters in *Basics 3*. You'll see that the same general sort of approach was used by Freddy—an ostinato-type melody over a 12-bar blues. The brief improvising in [B] makes use of Clapton's patented minor/major pentatonic mixing. Be aware of both sounds in this section as well as the other solos in the tune. He plays largely in the open and lower positions in open E form (*Basics 3*: Ch. 4), D form (*Basics 3*: Ch. 5) and C form (*Basics 3*: Ch. 2).

The ensemble figure in Interlude 1 [C] is very similar to the open and movable riffs we covered in *Basics 1* (Ch. 3) and *Basics 2* (Ch. 3). If you have any trouble with this line be sure to review those chapters.

Solo 1 [D] teems with definitive Claptonisms–blues lines distinguished by his aggressive attack, characteristic string bends and vibrato, bent double-stops and impeccable phrasing. Like the guitar work in "Crossroads" (see *Power Studies* 1), it laid the foundation for today's rock solo styles. It is played exclusively in the E form (*Basics 3*: Ch. 4) "blues box", a typical concession to the blues guitar heritage.

The first break [E] is begun with a fanfare on an E9—the "Hideaway chord," to quote Johnny Winter. The parallel sixth double-stops that follow are a little tricky since they are fingered on the 1st and 3rd strings and move down the fretboard rapidly.

Use hybrid picking or finger picking (*Basics 2*: Ch. 5) to articulate the sixth diads and learn the shapes separately at first. Be aware of common physical shapes. Combine all the positions only after you can make a series of smooth connections with one or two position changes in a group. This will help you build up the physical and visualizing technique necessary to nail them effortlessly every time. A combination of pentatonic forms is used throughout the remainder of the section—E minor form, C form, A minor form (*Basics 3*: Ch. 2) and C minor form (*Basics 3*: Ch. 7). Also check out *Basics 3*: Ch. 7 for connecting forms.

Interlude 2 [F] switches to a contrasting straight-8th feel. Here, open and movable riffs are moved through the 12-bar progression. See *Basics 1*: Ch. 5 and *Basics 2*: Ch. 3). The triplet feel shuffle groove is recalled for the rest of "Hideaway." The fiery solo at [G] is played entirely in the E form (a la "Crossroads") and uses the mixture of E minor and major pentatonic sounds. The string bending in bars 4-6 will demand a little extra technique work. This is all played with a one-finger (index) bend which requires more strength to accomplish since no additional reinforcement fingers are available to help push the string.

The head out [I] restates the main theme with variations in the E and D minor forms (*Basics 3*: Ch. 4). Notice the skillful improvising blended with allusions to the theme's melody.

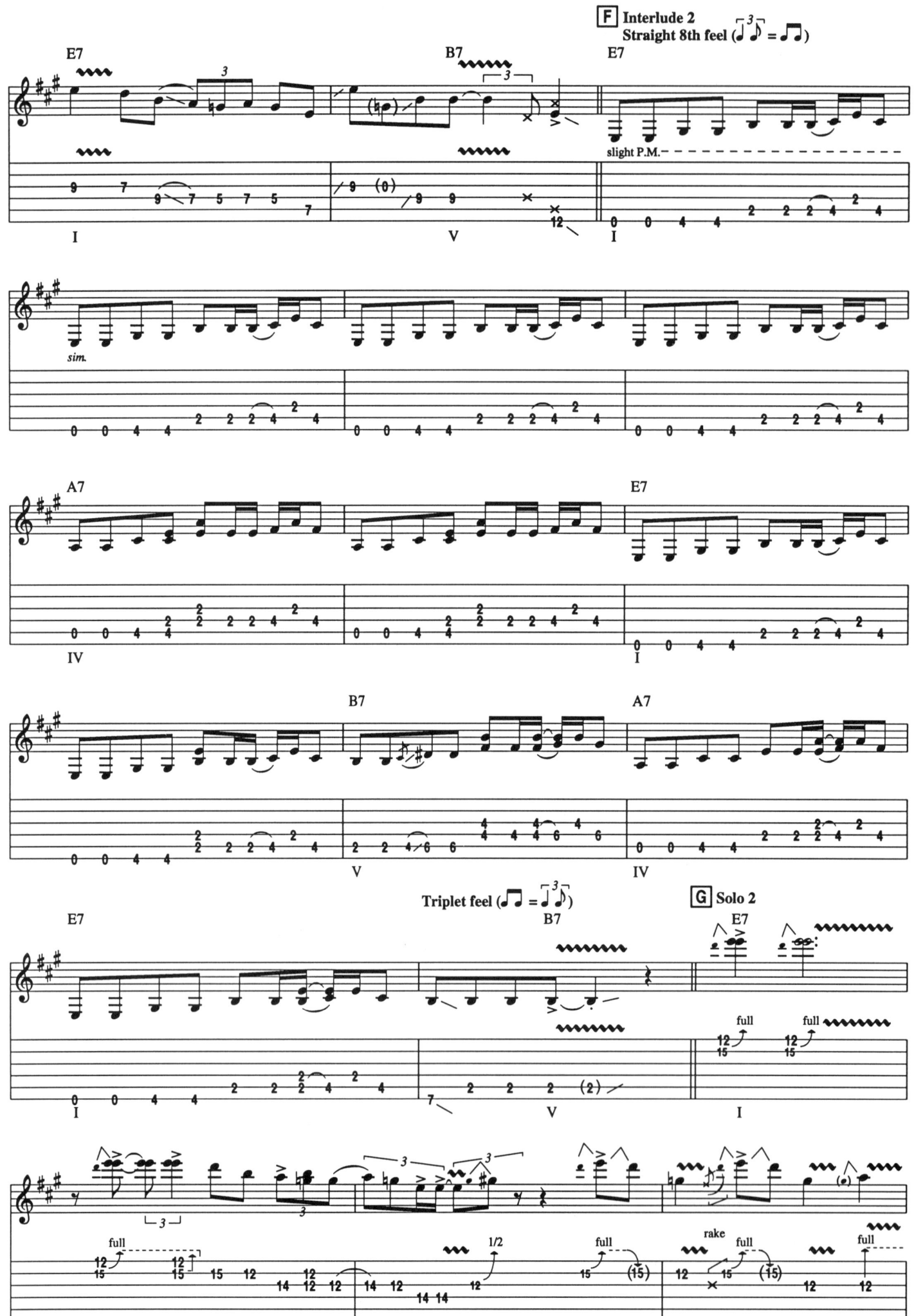

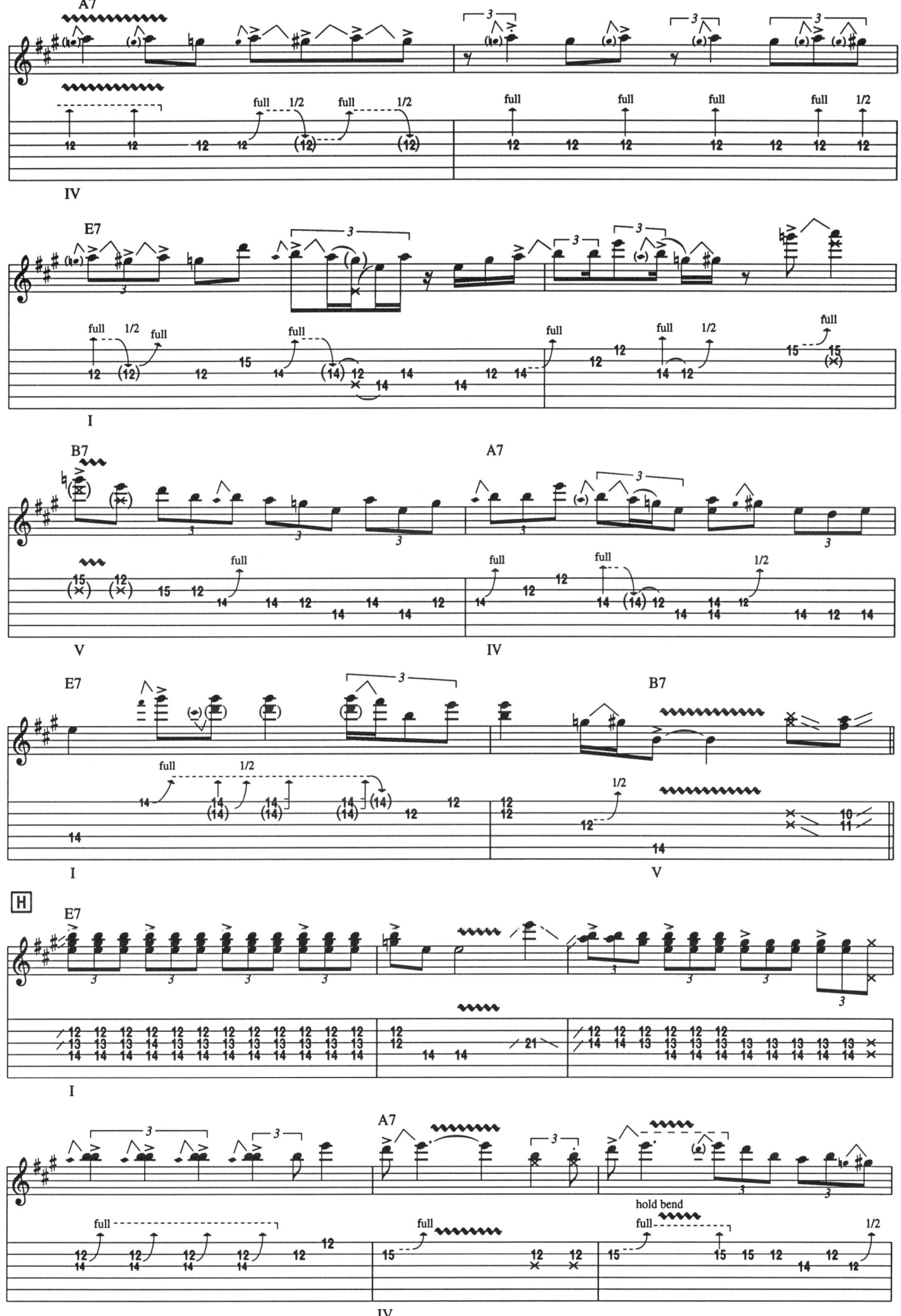

CRAZY TRAIN
Ozzy Osbourne

Ozzy and Black Sabbath may have invented the ultra-heavy, dungeonistic branch of metal some ten years earlier but his 1980 *Blizzard of Ozz* band with Randy Rhoads virtually cleared the decks and reinvented the genre. More than historically important, the well-known Osbourne/Rhoads collaboration "Crazy Train" contains many of the trademark elements that made up Randy's style and influenced the course of hard rock and metal music in the 1980's.

The memorable riff in the intro [A] is a diatonic/modal line. (For more on the subject of modes see *Advanced Concepts and Techniques*.) The riff is in F# minor. Play it as an introduction to modes and realize that it is a typical Aeolian Mode melody. For now use your current tools to get a handle on it. Visualize the F#5 power chord as you play the riff and see it as the underlying shape behind the riff. This is also a great line to reinforce the power chord scale relationship.

Rhy. Fig. 1, used throughout verses [B], is definitive Rhoads. It is made from familiar ingredients— triads over an open A pedal point. Driven by a chugging 16th-note groove, it is a staple of modern metal. Relate the triad shapes to their larger parent chords in *Basics 3*. For example, A in the fifth position is from the E form (*Basics 3*: Ch. 4), and E and D are from the C form (*Basics 3*: Ch. 2). (Look for more on triads in *Advanced Concepts and Techniques*.) The patented open position pull-off scale line played before the verses serves a good introduction to basic diatonic scale sounds. The strong, inventive accompaniment figures in the chorus [C] combine movable and open chord forms. (See *Basics 1* and *Basics 2*). This is a textbook example of a well-constructed hard rock/heavy metal rhythm part. In the first chorus, the F# minor fill between phrases is based directly on the open E minor form (*Basics 3*: Ch. 1).

Randy's guitar solo [E] is more advanced than most we've looked at so far. As with other difficult solos in the *Power Studies* series, begin by playing the rhythm part (Gtr. 1 in slashes) behind the solo and get the sound and feel of the phrases in your ears. Then approach it carefully learning and practicing the phrases gradually until the motor skills and technique develop. It would be helpful to review Van Halen's solo in "You Really Got Me" from *Power Studies 2* for tap-on technique.

Tap-on lines outline the backing chord changes, F# minor and D major in the first two bars. Bends and tap-ons are found in the next measure. Put these bars together slowly, focusing on accuracy. Some of the diatonic scale licks are easier and more accessible like the melodious lines in bars 5 and 6. You can easily relate these to the E minor form in *Basics 3*: Ch. 1. Others will bear resemblance to pentatonic licks you already know—like the ones in bars 7-9 and bars 13-15. These are clearly in our E minor blues-box form seen in the movable lead patterns in Chapter 4 of *Basics 2*. The tricky diatonic run which is the solo's climax will be in your grasp after you work on the modes in *Advanced Concepts and Techniques*. For now work on it slowly, breaking down the long line into bite-sized pieces. Here's a suggestion. Take each 3-to-a-string pattern and learn it separately before joining the patterns together. Then take two or three strings' worth (four to six patterns) of music at a time and practice that much. Finally play the whole phrase slowly, concentrating on your hammer-on technique and smooth connections in position changing. As you improve in practice, gradually bring up the tempo making certain the notes remain clean and precise. This is particularly important when playing with the sort of ultra-distorted metal tone that Randy used.

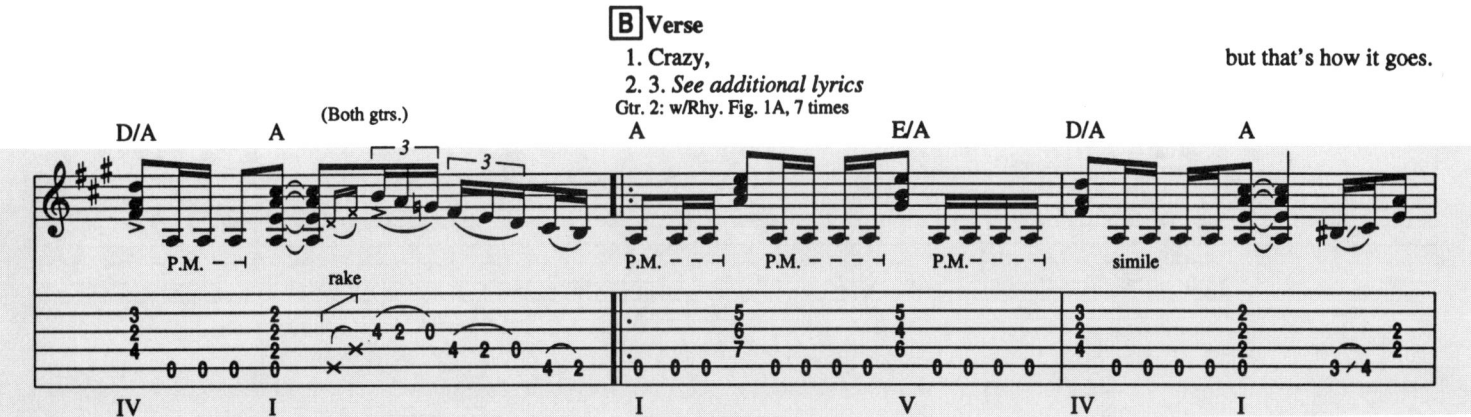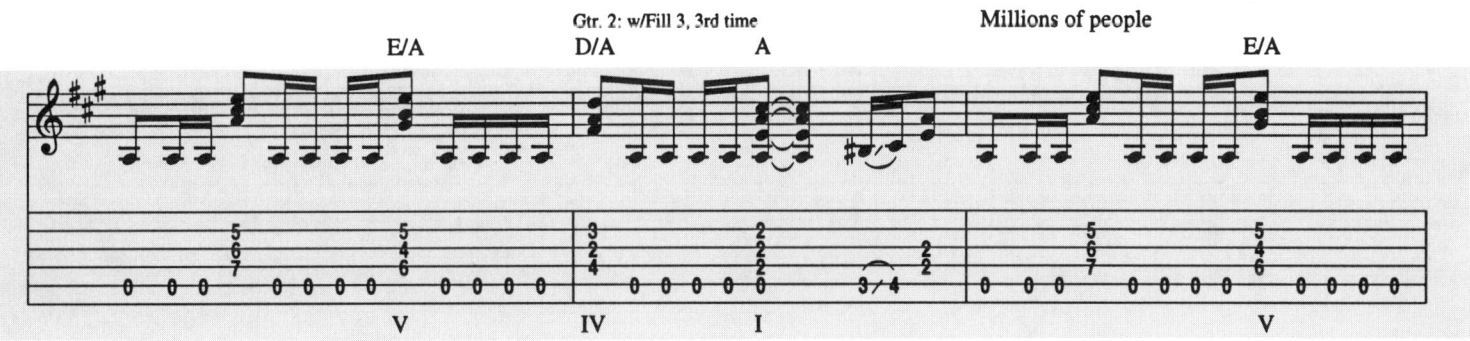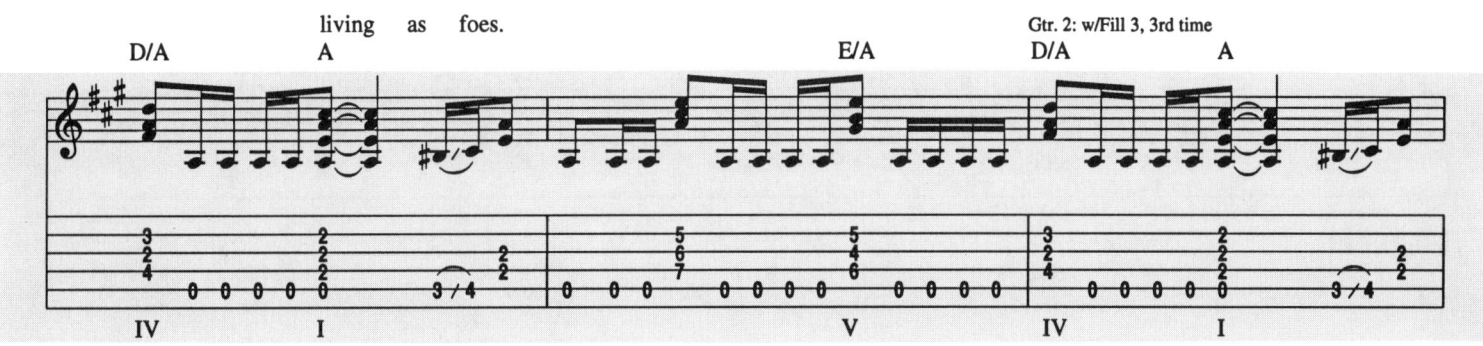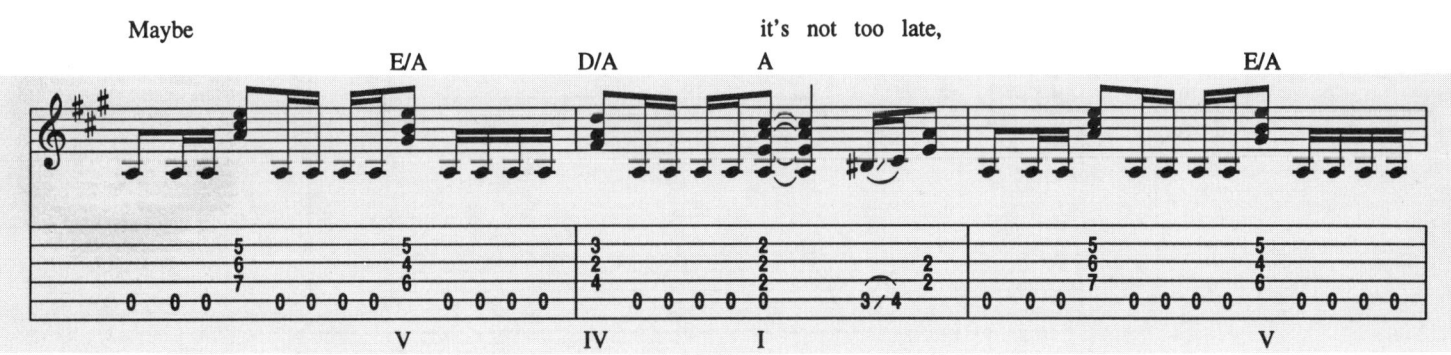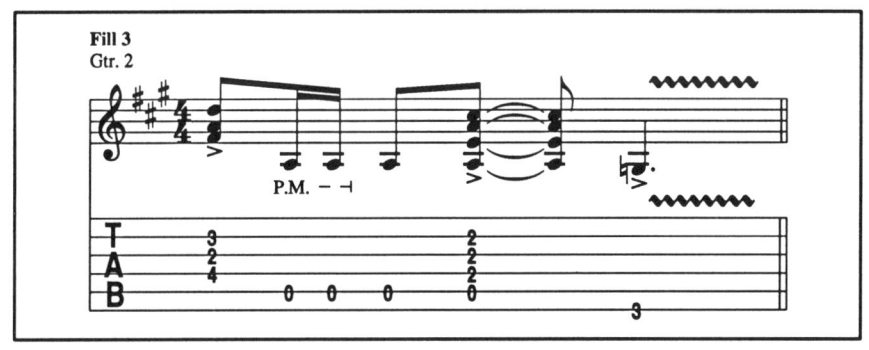

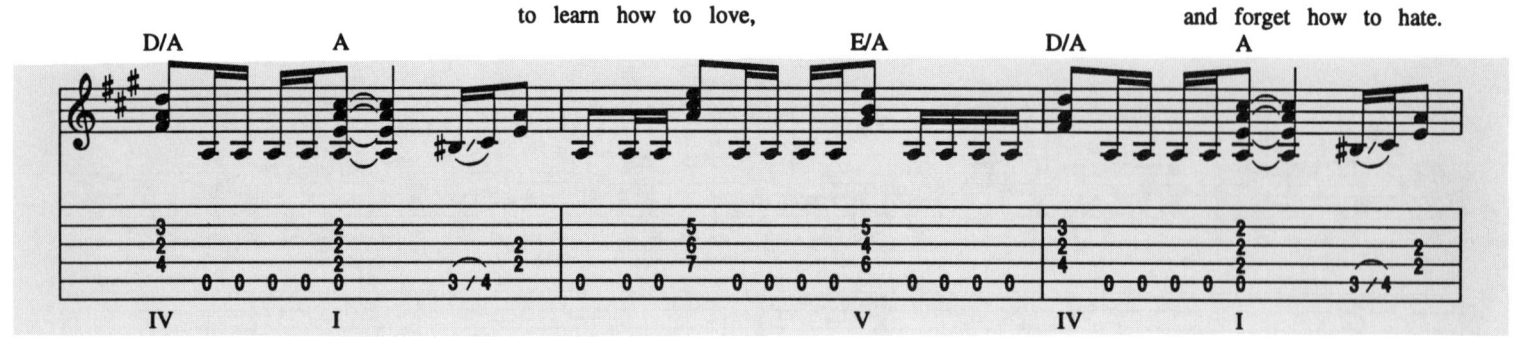
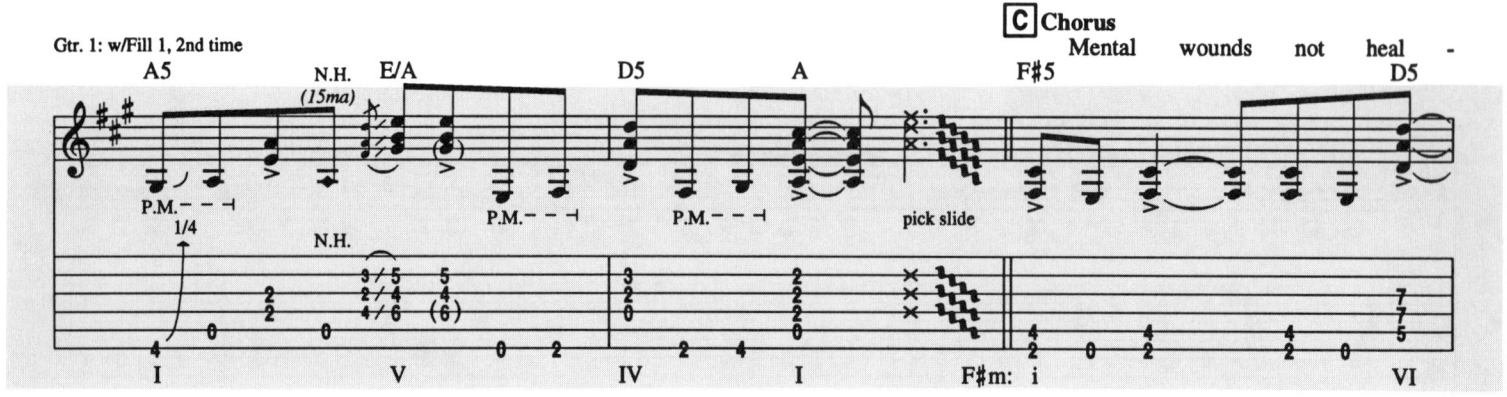
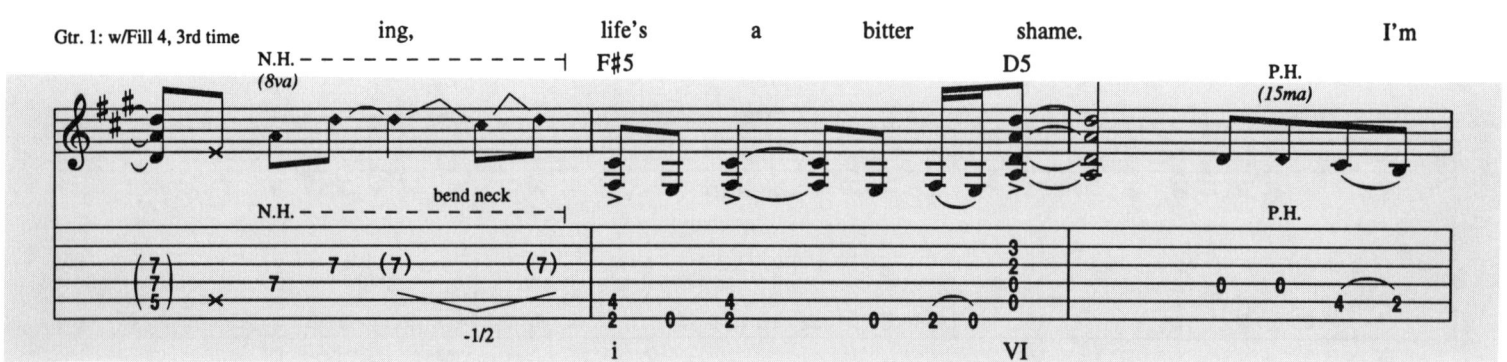
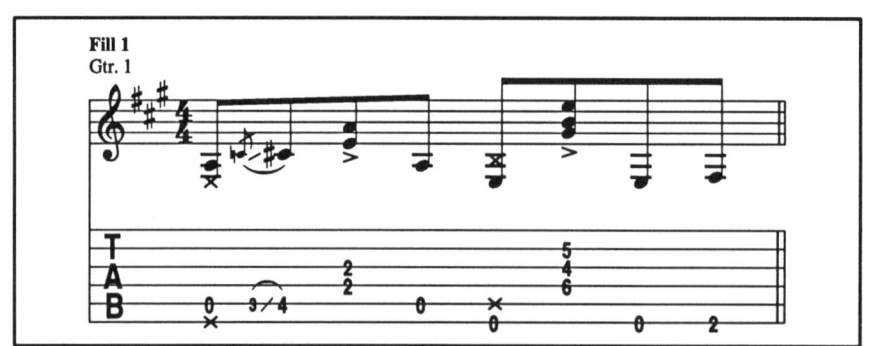
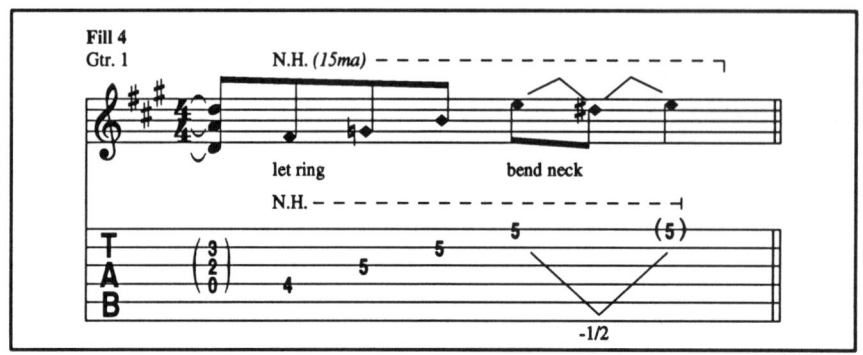

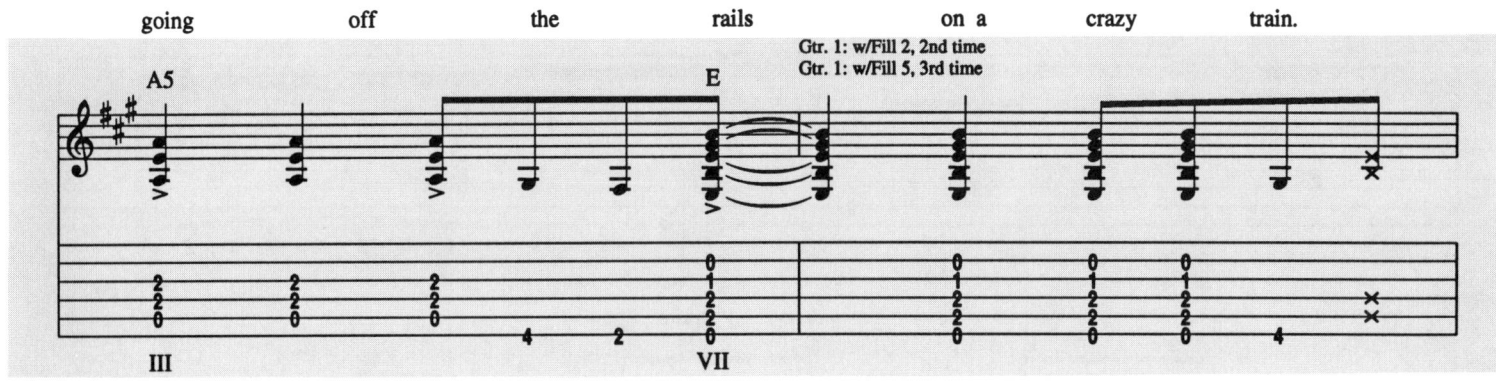
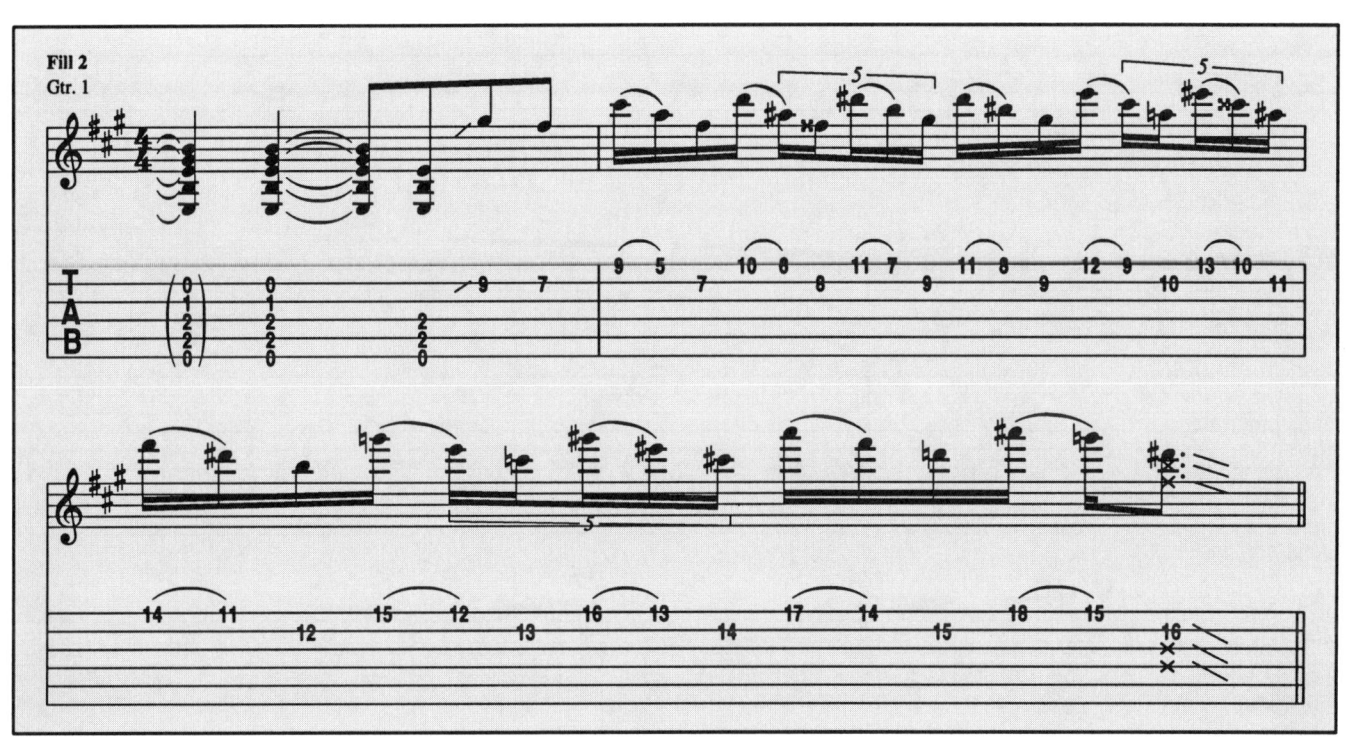
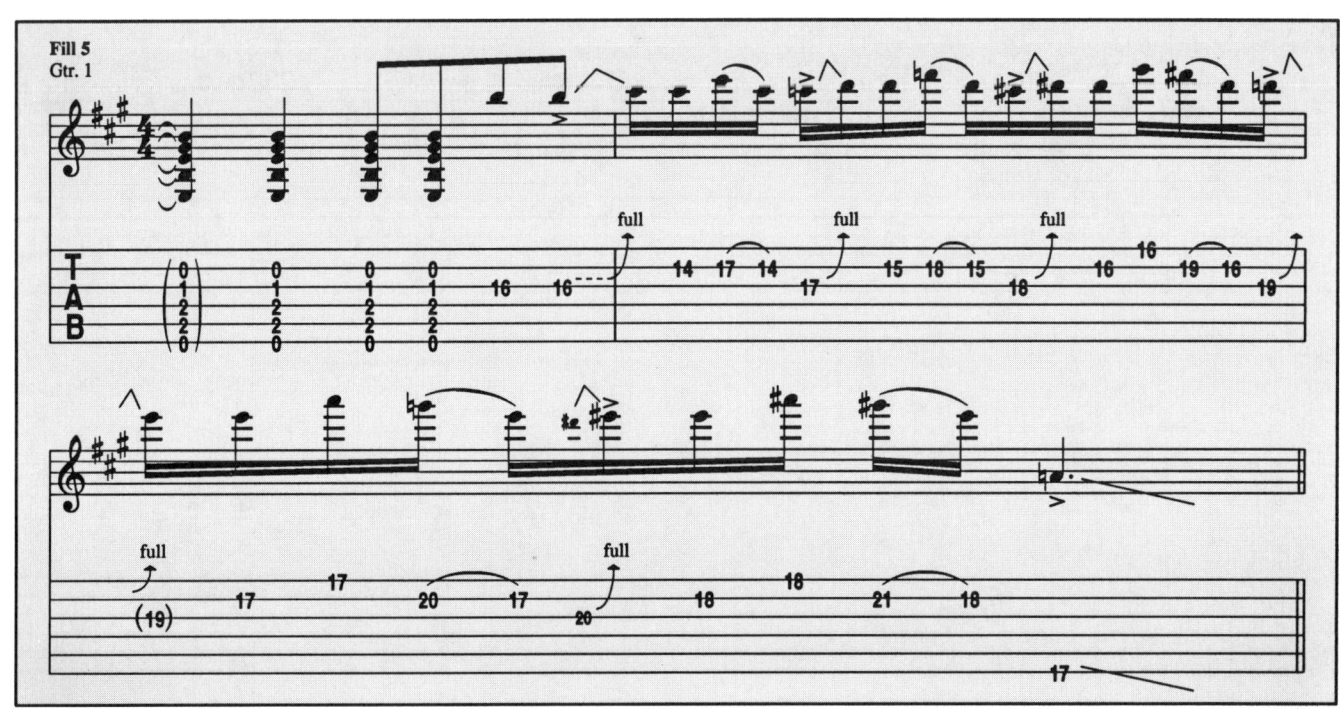

51

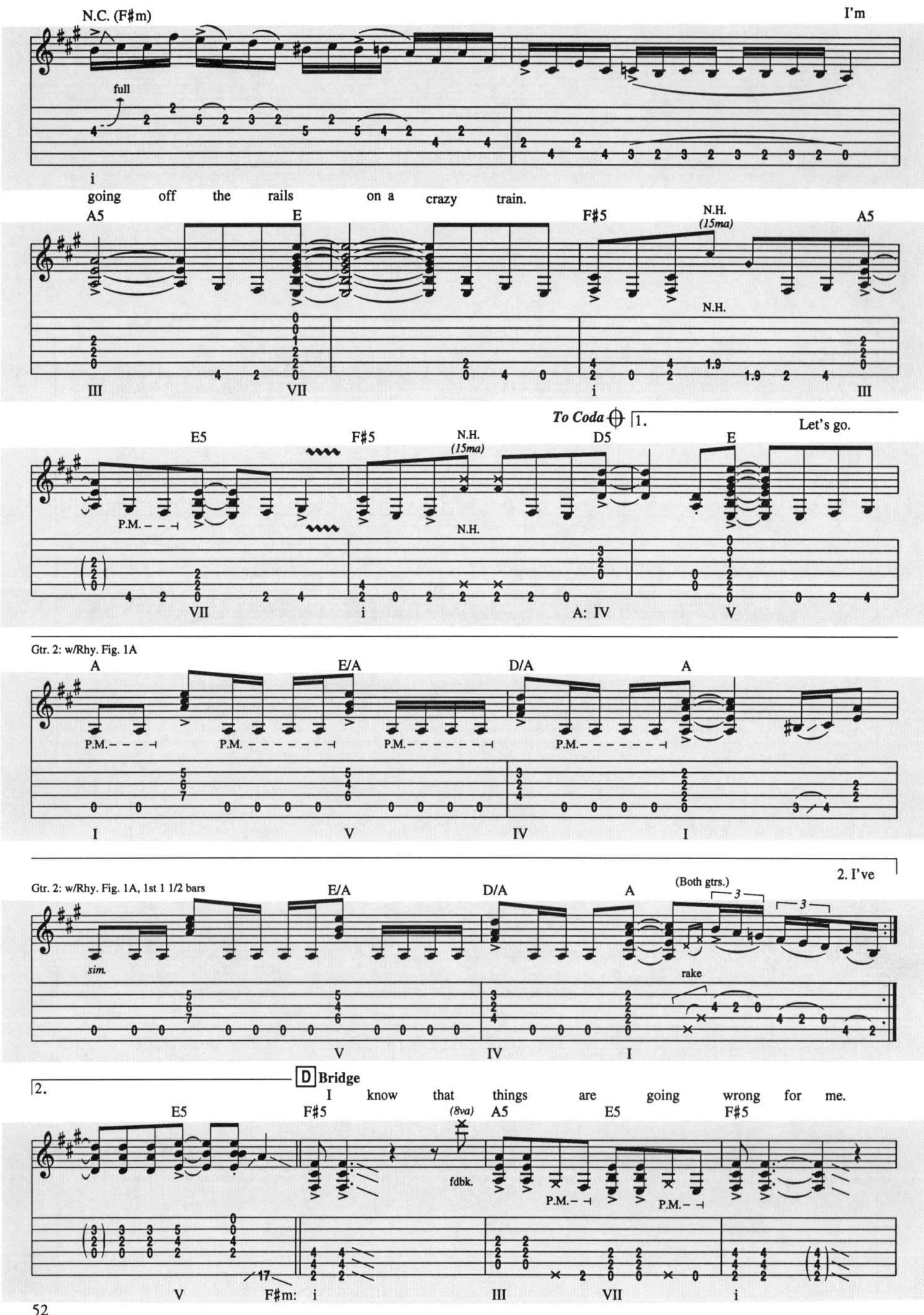

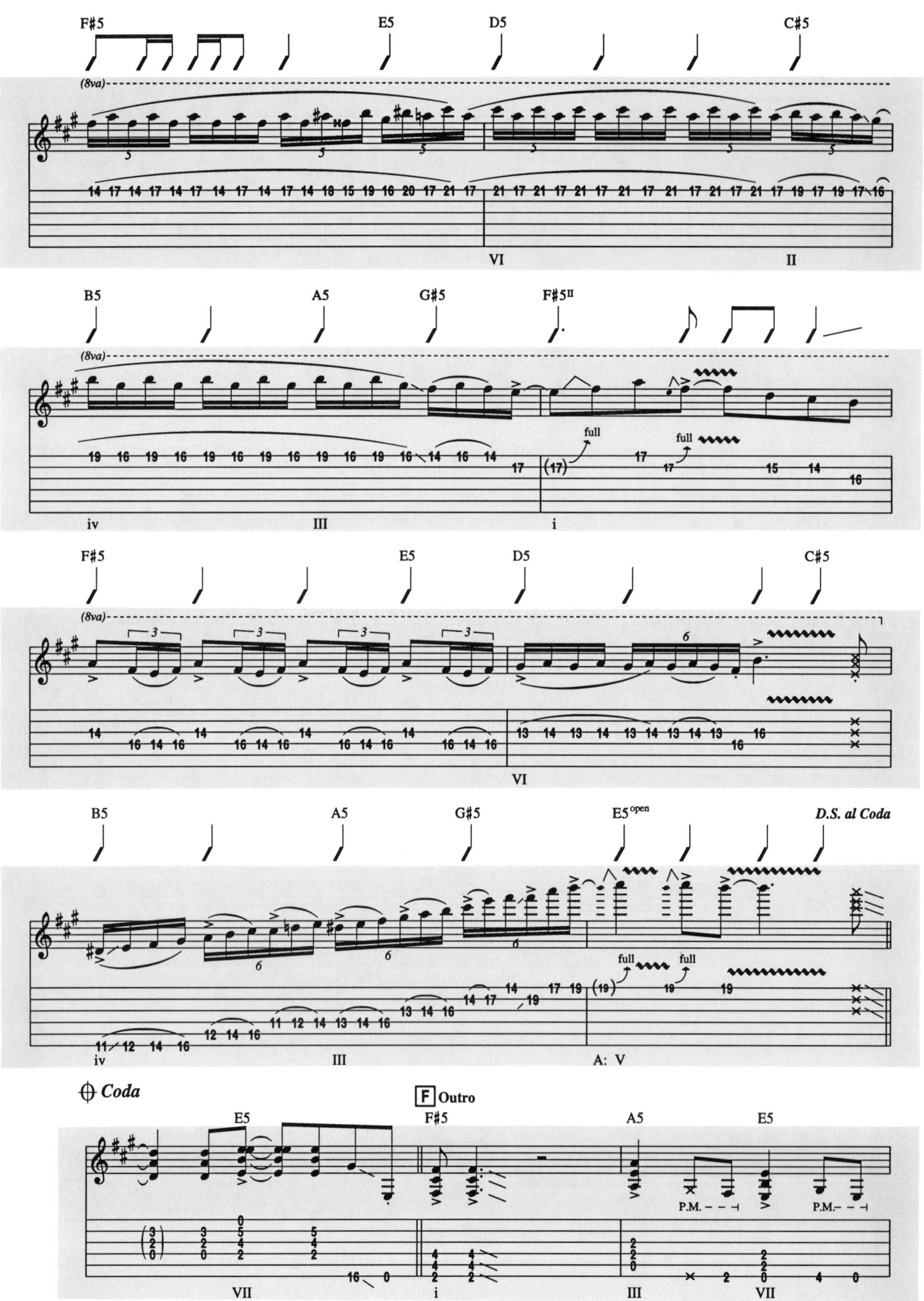

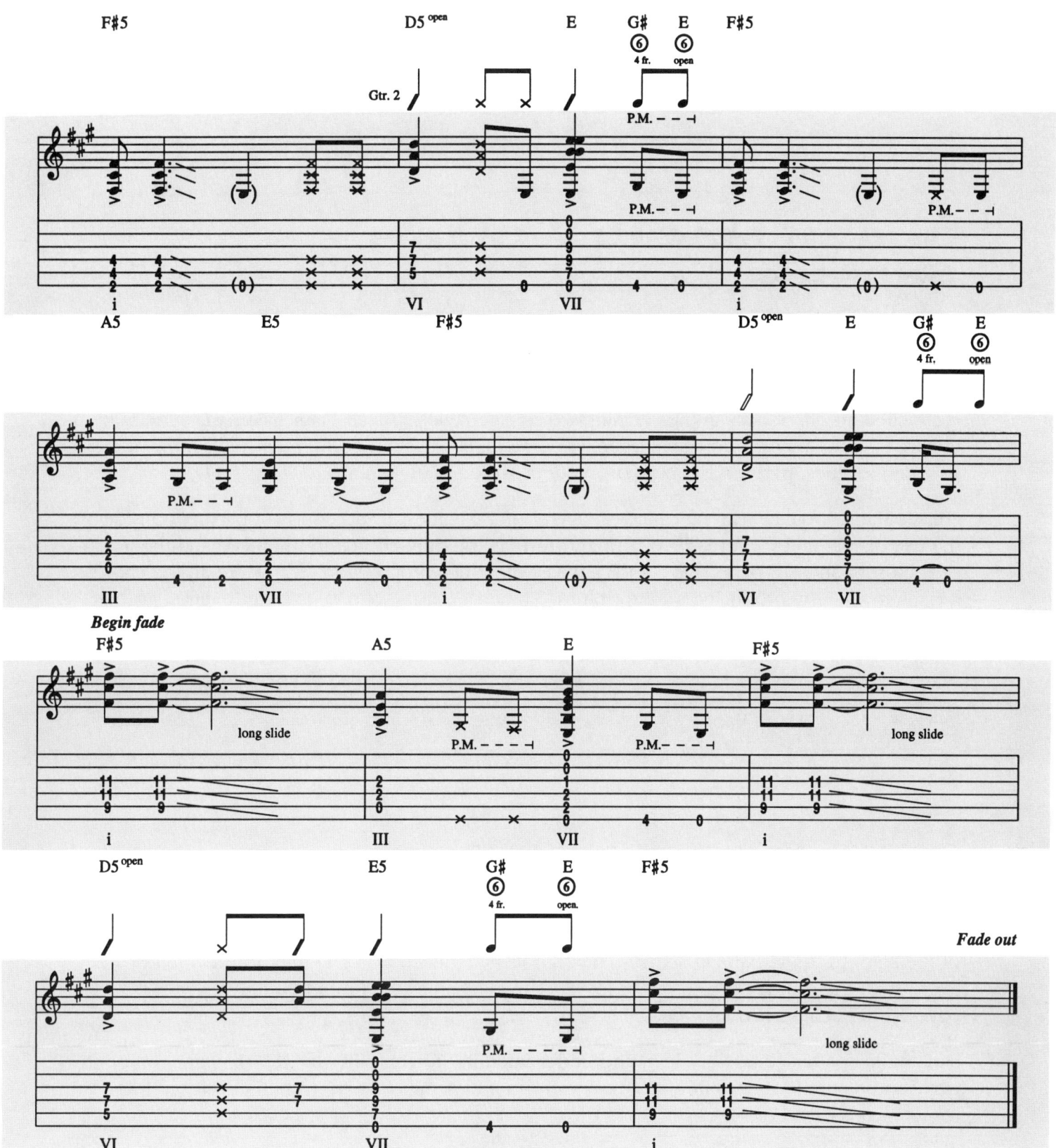

Additional lyrics

2. I've listened to preachers, I've listened to fools.
   I've watched all the dropouts who make their own rules.
   One person conditioned to rule and control,
   The media sells it and you live the role.

   (Chorus 2)
   Mental wounds still screaming, driving me insane.
   I'm going off the rails on a crazy train. *(2 times)*

3. Heirs of a cold war, that's what we've become.
   Inheriting troubles, I'm mentally numb.
   Crazy, I just cannot bear.
   I'm living with something that just isn't fair.

   (Chorus 3)
   Mental wounds not healing, who and what's to blame.
   I'm going off the rails on a crazy train. *(2 times)*

BLACK MAGIC WOMAN
Santana

Spawned in the late 1960's San Francisco psychedelic hippie scene, Santana was unique in its day, and remains so to the present. An ambitious experiment of guitarist Carlos Santana, the group personified the term eclectic blending rock, jazz, latin and blues music and effectively reconciled all differences in the seemingly disparate styles. "Black Magic Woman," written by guitarist Peter Green (John Mayall/Fleetwood Mac), is a case in point. Elusively simple, it is a part minor blues, part modal jazz, part modern rock and all Santana.

"Black Magic Woman" can be called an altered minor blues. If this sounds obscure, consider the use of i, iv and v chords (Dm, Gm and Am) as the only chords in the piece and the length of each section is 12 bars. This is indicative of the blues progression (B1). Here all the chords are minor thereby producing a minor blues The order of the chords is slightly different than standard 12-bar blues hence the altered blues. Here's a chart of the basic form.

i	i	v	v	\\i	i	iv	iv	\\i	v	i	i
Dm		Am			Dm		Gm		Dm	Am	Dm

The intro [A] begins with subtle minor mode lines. These are quite accessible and serve as an ideal introduction to diatonic minor scale sounds. The lines are centered around the Am form (*Basics 3*: Ch. 2). The arpeggiated Dm chord leads to the intro solo [B]. Carlos improvises in D minor pentatonic in the open E minor "blues box" form (*Basics 3*: Ch. 1) for the first six bars of the solo. In the remaining six bars, he combines connections of D minor and G minor forms with the "home base" E minor form. (The mechanics of combining minor forms is covered in detail in *Basics 3*: Ch. 7.)

Santana keeps his guitarwork lean and understated in the verses [C] [D] [F]. His light comping is based on simple shapes in open E minor form and A minor form. (Again check out the forms in *Basics 3*: Ch. 7.)

The solo [E] finds Carlos building his lines almost exclusively in the blues-oriented boxes of the E minor (*Basics 3*: Ch. 1) and D minor (*Basics 3*: Ch. 4) forms. Check out his signature string bends, vibrato and his frequent melodic use of the ninth, E, as an added tone to the minor pentatonic scale. (See "Another Brick in the Wall, Part II" and "Lenny" elsewhere in *Power Studies 3* for other examples of this typical addition to the minor pentatonic.) The important subject of adding other tones to the pentatonic will be pursued in greater detail in *Advanced Concepts and Techniques*.

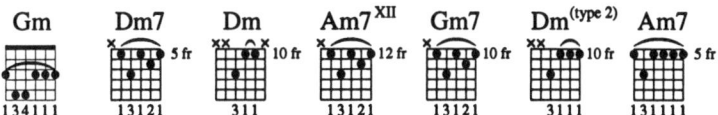

Black Magic Woman

Words and Music by Peter Green

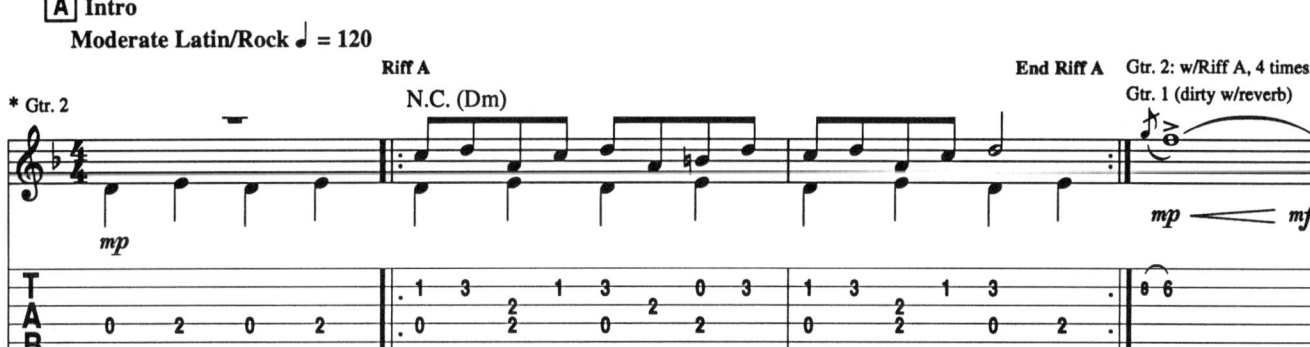

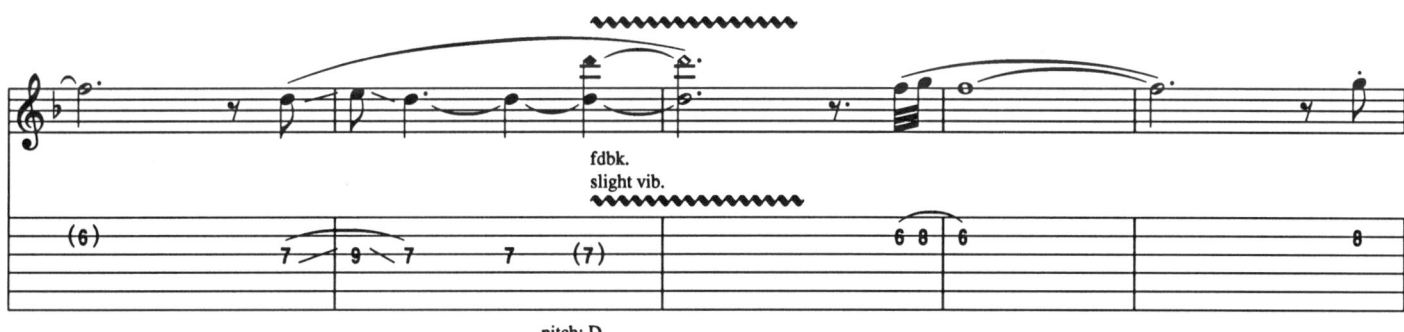

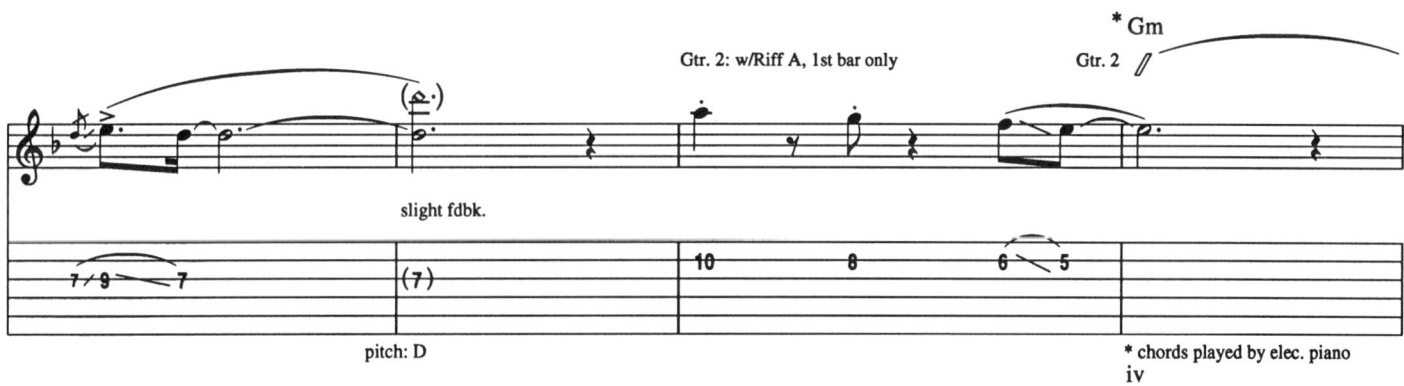

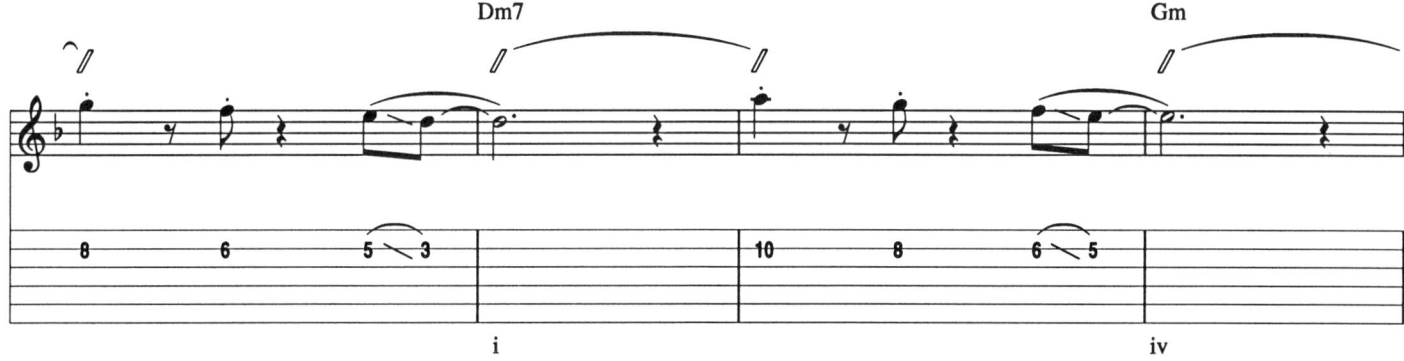

Copyright © 1968 and 1980 by King Publishing Co. Ltd., London, England
All Rights for the U.S.A. and Canada Controlled by Murbo Music Publishing Inc.
International Copyright Secured   All Rights Reserved

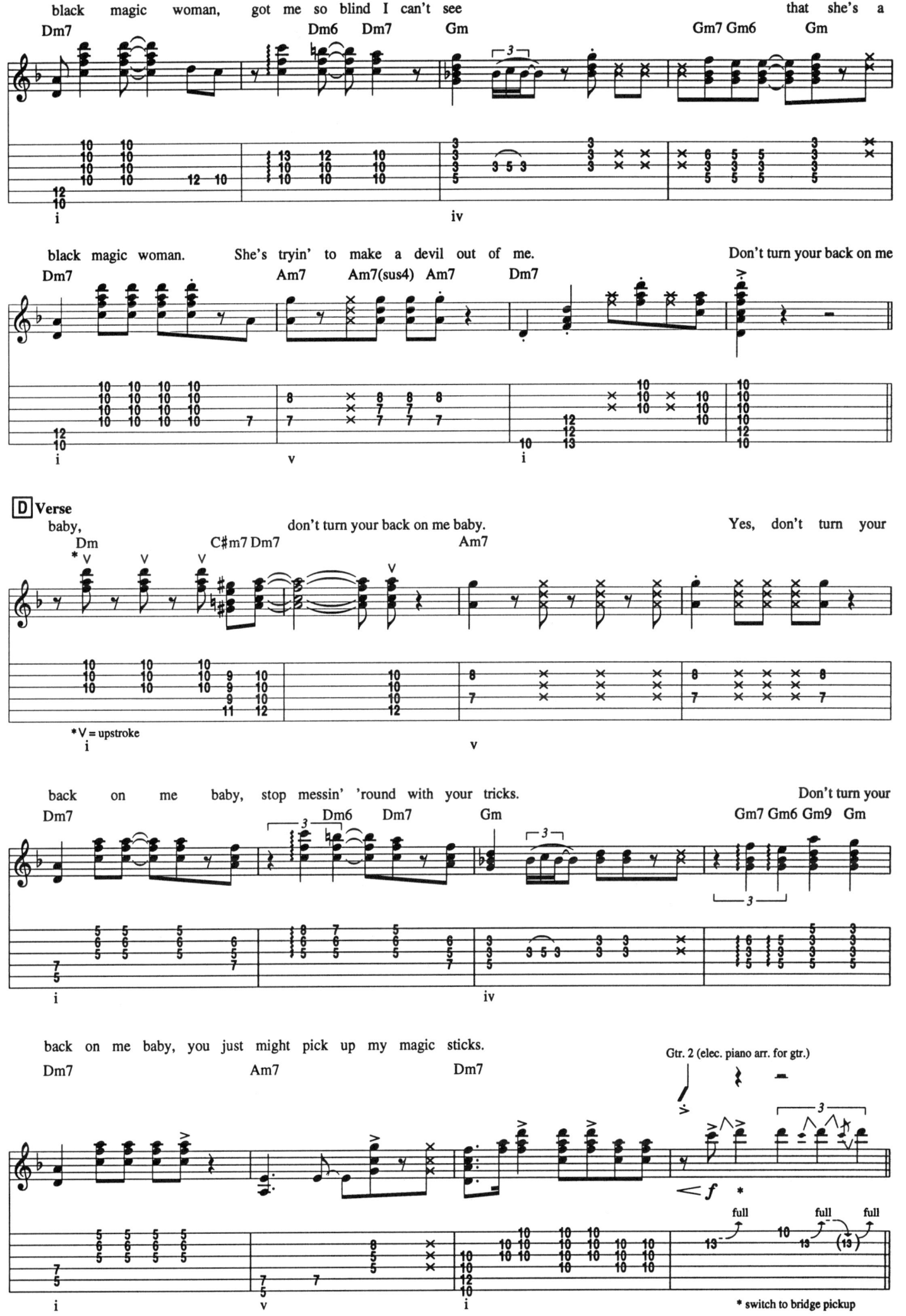

REELIN' IN THE YEARS
Steely Dan

On their 1972 debut album, *Can't Buy a Thrill*, Steely Dan was essentially a self-contained six-piece band. One notable exception is the participation of New York sessionman Elliott Randall, on "Reelin' in the Years," who was called in by long-time friend Jeff Baxter (then a member of Steely Dan). It was Elliott who played the memorable and stirring lead guitar lines on the track. Concerning rock playing, Elliott stated in a 1977 interview that two important factors in his style are knowing how to bend notes properly (intonation) and how to control tone at high volume (overdrive)—two elements clearly at work in his "Reelin' in the Years" solos.

The chord progression in the intro [A], choruses [C] [D] [G], interludes [E] [H], solo [F] and outro [I] is derived from an A Mixolydian mode tonal center and embodies the dominant changes of the song. The use of the recurring VII–I pattern (in this case, G–A in the tonal center of A major) is indigenous to rock—think of classics like "My Generation," "Shapes of Things" and "Freeway Jam" as just a handful of the countless tunes employing this common progression.

The intro guitar solo [A] finds Elliott (Gtr. 1) all over the neck in A major pentatonic. The lines combine the E form (*Basics 3*: Ch. 4), D form (*Basics 3*: Ch. 5) and G form (*Basics 3*: Ch. 1). Though predominately major pentatonic there are moments which combine major and minor sounds—a common aspect of the rock and blues idioms. (See "Sunshine of Your Love" elsewhere in this volume for more background.) The diatonic Mixolydian mode line in bars 12 and 13 makes a great study in the intervals of the mode. It's easy to visualize on the fretboard and to hear the individual steps as they are moved down in repeating patterns on the high E string. Gtr. 2 plays major pentatonic lines in G and A as accompaniment riffs behind the solo. These also heard in the choruses and outro in slightly varied forms. The figures are similar to and function like the movable riffs in *Basics 2*: Ch. 3. The first interlude [E] makes use of open position diatonic lines. The melodies are clearly scalar implying the A Mixolydian mode. Begin to train your ear for modes by playing the lines and listening to how they define the background G-A (VII–I) chord changes. The trickiest part of the section is in the second ending where quick pull-off riffs are found. Work on this measure slowly at first, concentrating on an even tempo, smooth legato technique and clarity. In his memorable guitar solo [F], Elliott works primarily out of the combined major pentatonic forms covered in *Basics 3*: Ch. 6. The individual forms used are the E form (*Basics 3*: Ch. 4), D form (*Basics 3*: Ch. 5), C form (*Basics 3*: Ch. 2) and A form (*Basics 3*: Ch. 3).

The outro guitar solo [I] begins with repeated major pentatonic motifs played in a continually shifting rhythm. This is a strong and effective musical tool used by countless improvisors in rock, blues, jazz, pop and country. The idea is simplicity itself. Create a motif and then place each of its repetitions on a different beat. Here it is first heard on beat 3, then on the *and* of 2, next on beat 1, then on beat 4 and so on. The hammer-on/pull-off pattern played in bars 5-8 is an early jazz/rock/blues guitar cliché transplanted into a progressive rock setting. In fact, Les Paul played similar licks in the 1940's as did Cliff Gallup in the 1950's. Throughout the solo, Elliott alternates between major and minor sounds emphasizing parallel minor as in the aforementioned lick. (See parallel minor, *Basics 3*: Ch. 7.)

Solos like the one "Reelin' in the Years" are ideal for developing the ear to hear major/minor scale combining. Along similar lines, be sure to check out "Sunshine of Your Love," "You Shook Me" and "Lenny" in this volume as well as "You Really Got Me," "Crossroads," "Walk This Way," "Get Back" and "All Right Now" in *Power Studies 1* and *2*. Also see *Advanced Concepts and Techniques* for more on scale combining.

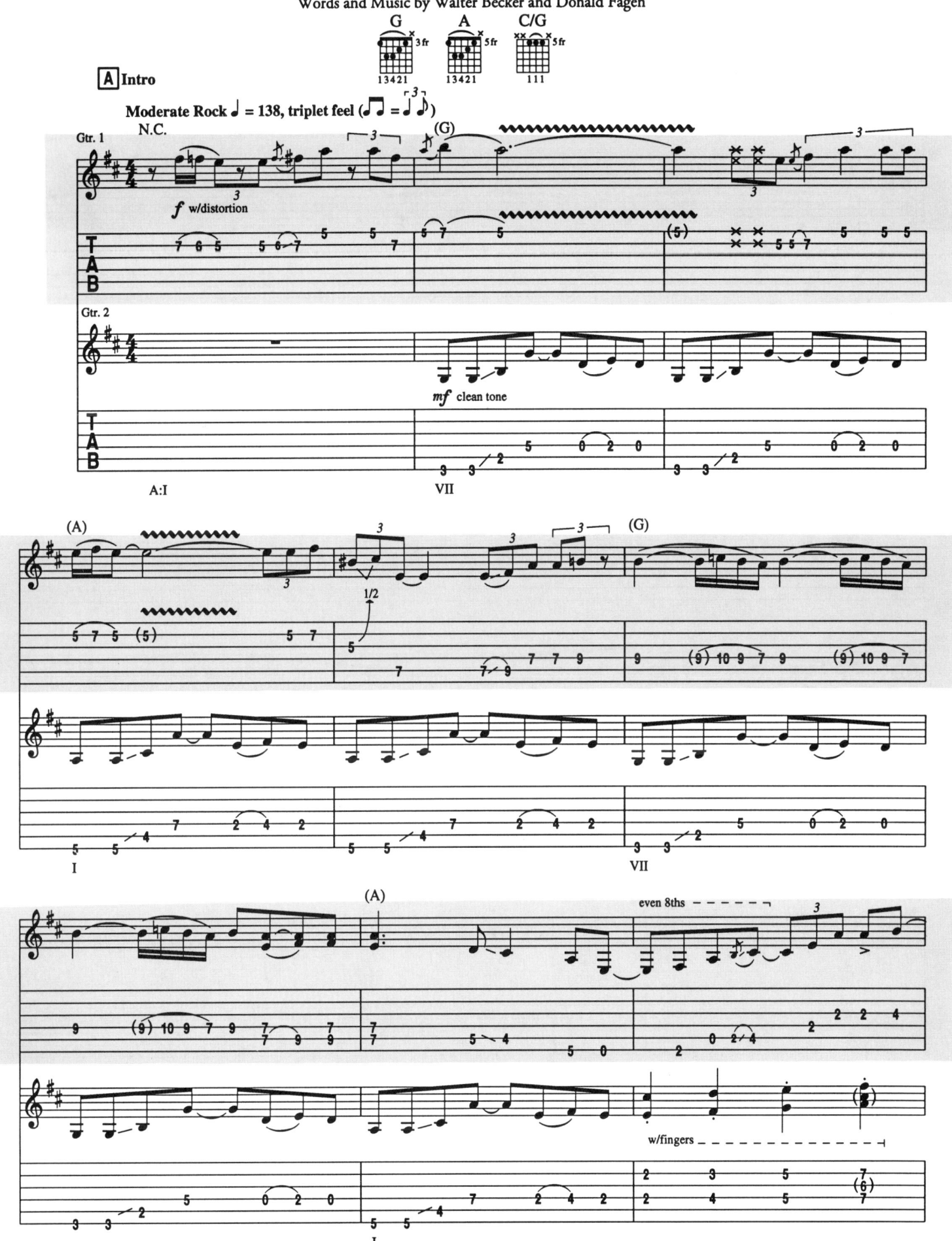

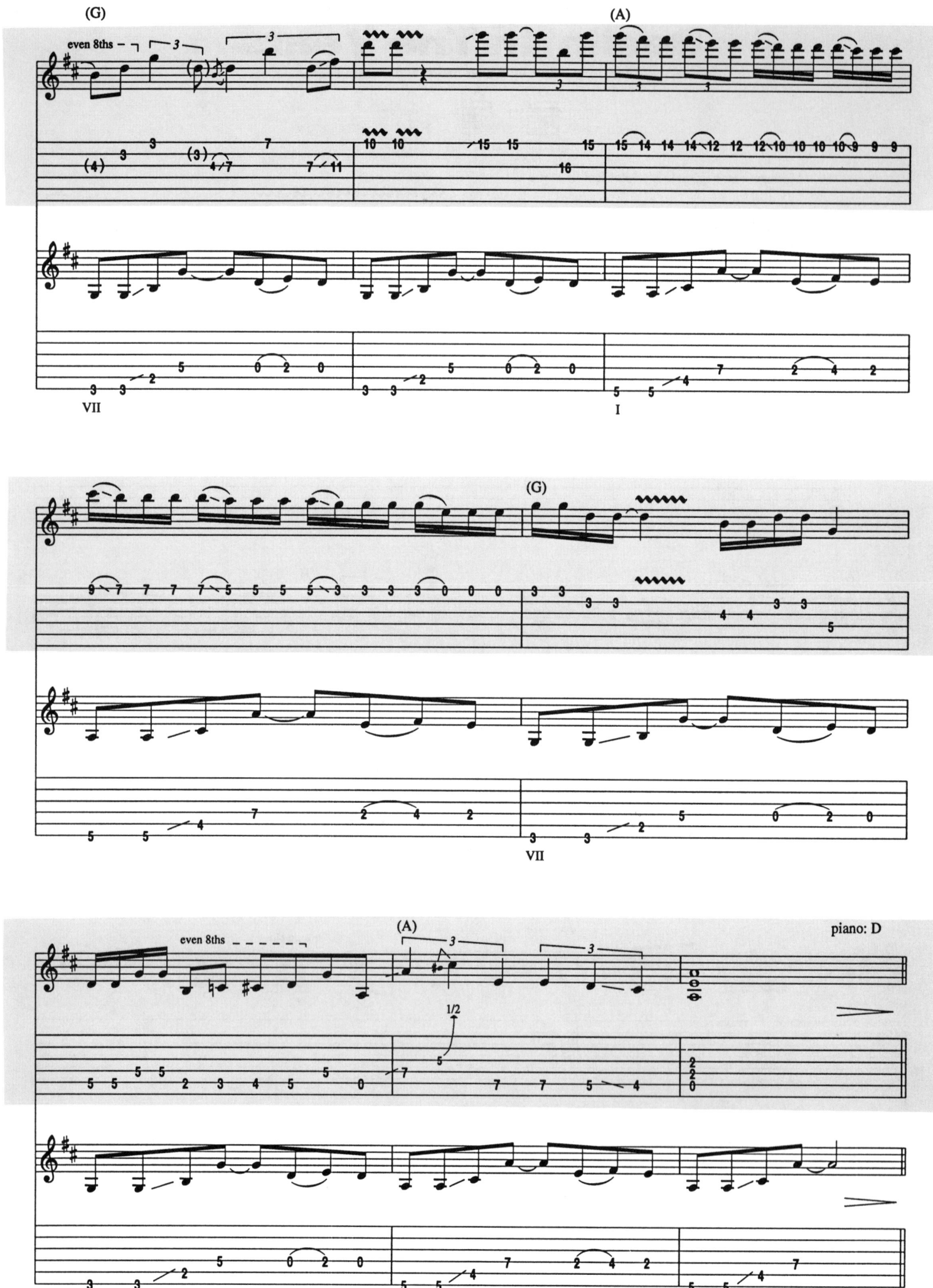

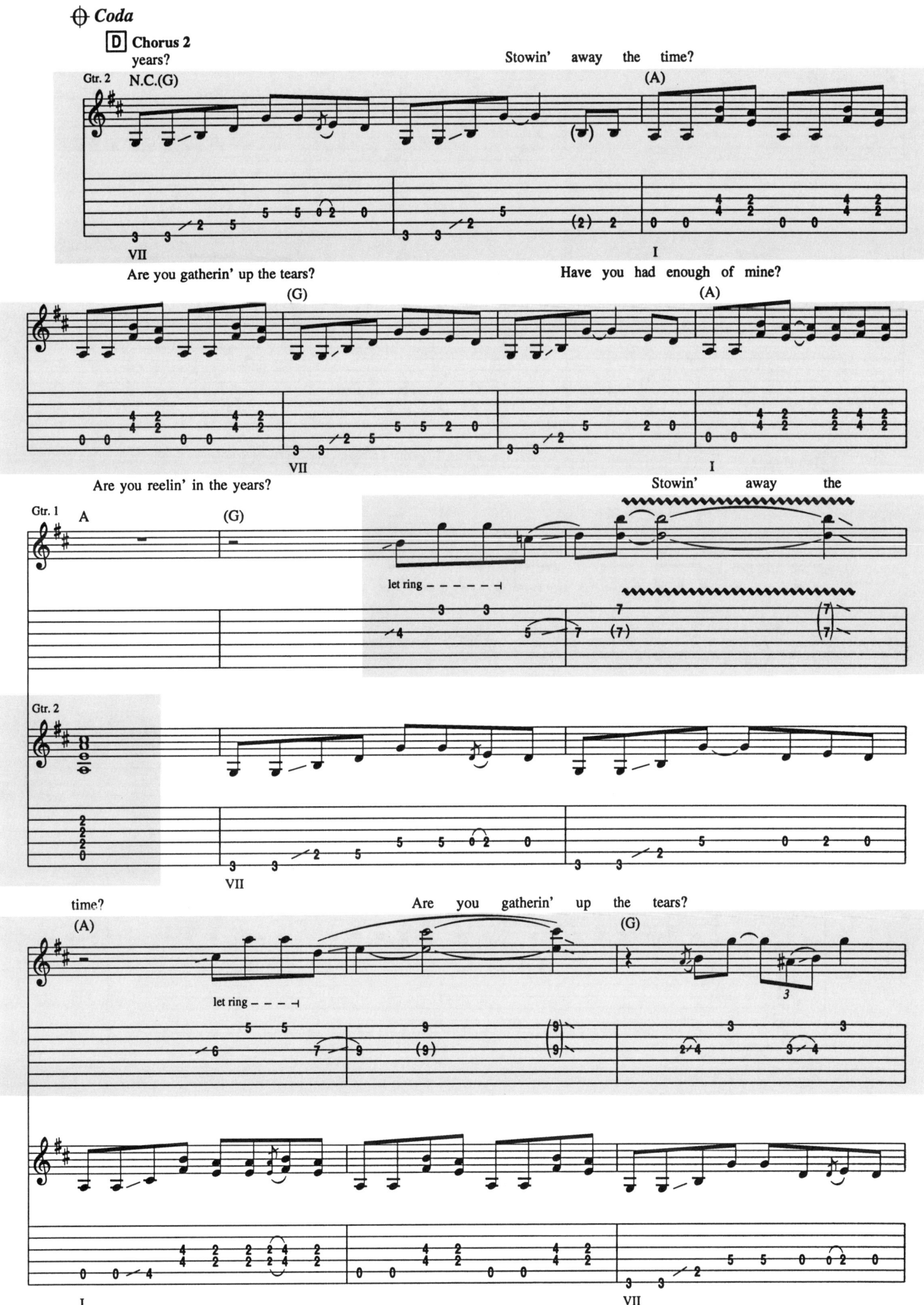

Have you had enough of mine?

E Interlude 1

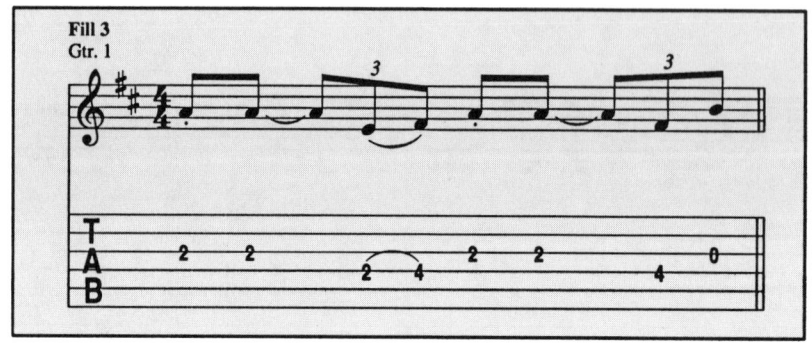

1.
2. Gtr. 3: w/Fill 4
End Rhy. Fig. 1
G
A
3fr
5fr
Gtr. 2: w/Rhy. Fig. 1
Gtr. 1
(G)
Gtr. 3
VII
(A)
I

Fill 4
Gtr. 3 (harmony)
T
A
B

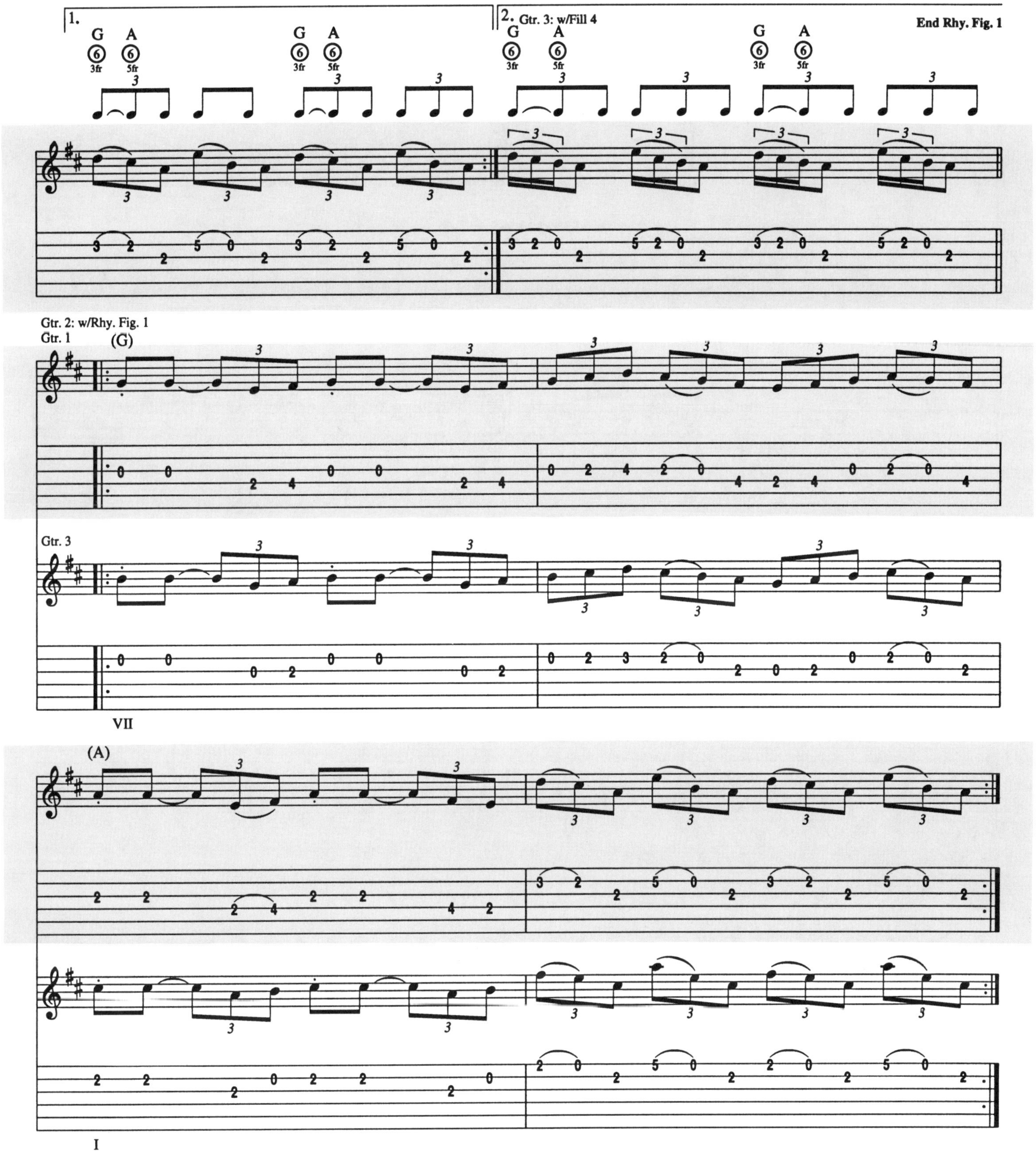

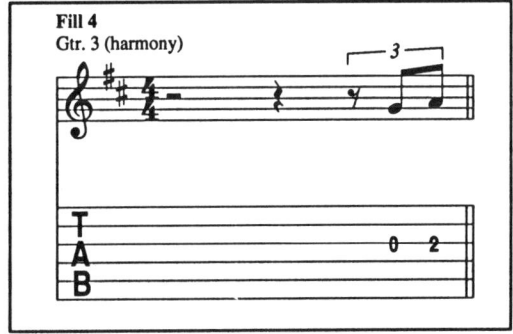

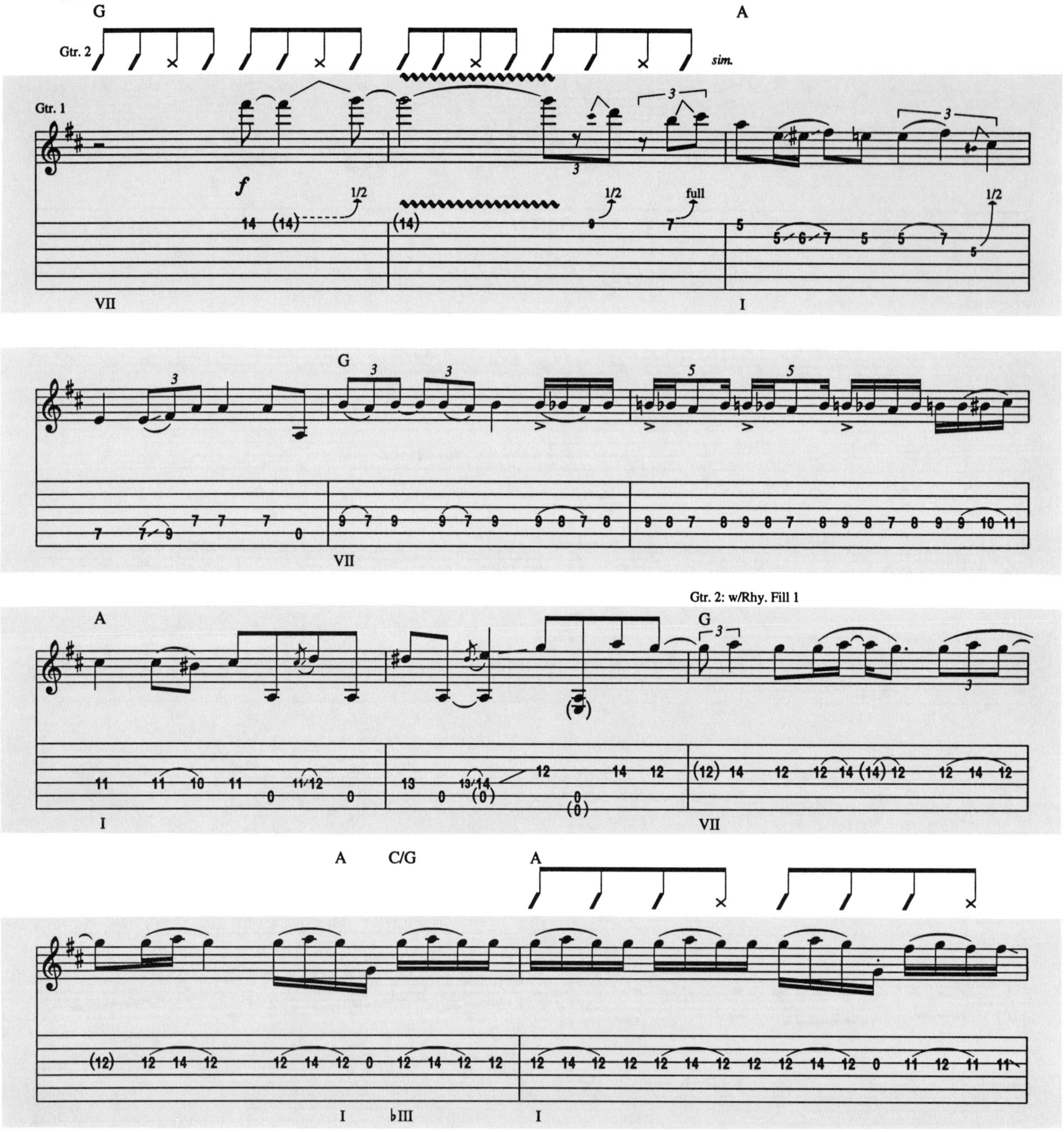

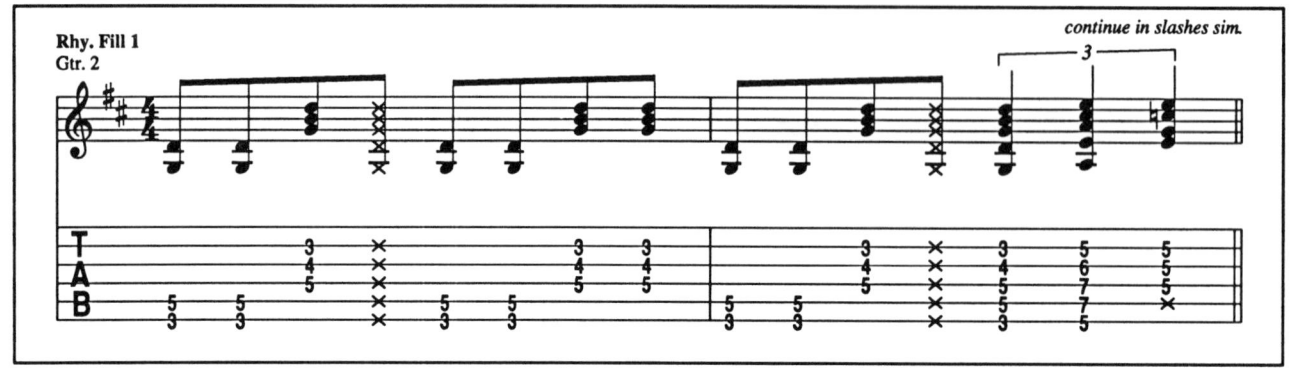

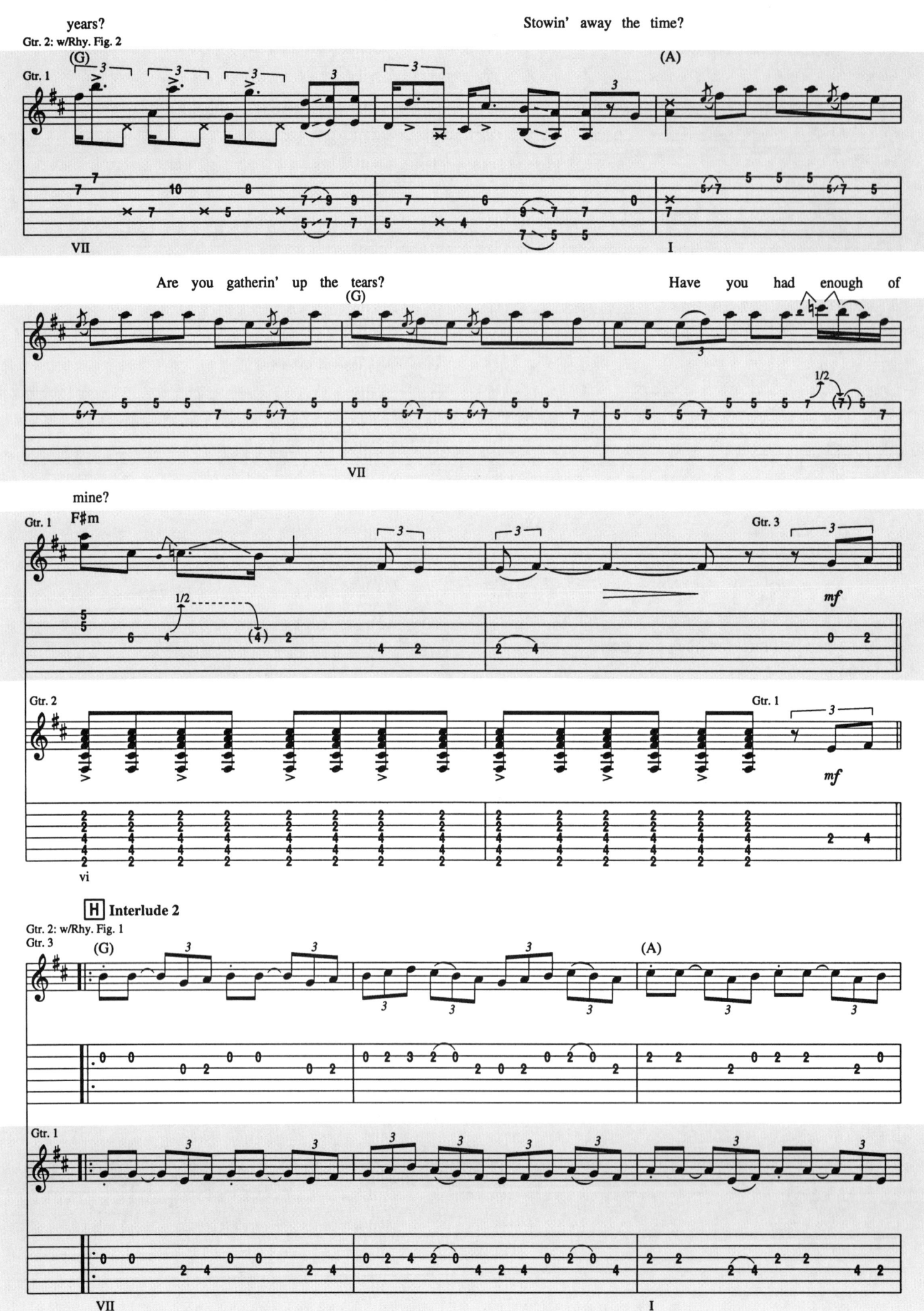

Additional lyrics

2. You've been tellin' me you're a genius since you were seventeen.
   In all the time I've known you I still don't know what you mean.
   The weekend at the college didn't turn out like you planned,
   The things that pass for knowledge I can't understand.
   (Chorus 2)

3. I've spent a lot of money and I've spent a lot of time.
   The trip we made to Hollywood is etched upon my mind.
   After all the things we've done and seen you find another man,
   The things you think are useless I can't understand.
   (Chorus 3)

ANOTHER BRICK IN THE WALL, PART 2
Pink Floyd

Born of late '60's psychedelia, British blues and space rock, Pink Floyd occupies a unique place in the annals of contemporary music history. A cult band with an enormous mass audience, they have endured in spite of the varied trends and fickle tastes of the 1970's. After a string of adventurous records, their 1979 conceptual double-album effectively closed out the decade and produced their biggest (and often deemed best) hit, "Another Brick in the Wall, Part 2." Regarded as one of guitarist David Gilmour's finest moments, it combines the trademark Floydian elements of progressive rock, pop, R&B and musique concrete creating an ideal setting for his sonic explorations.

Let's examine the way Gilmour approaches the guitarwork in this piece. Two guitars are involved in the verses [A]. Gtr. 1 plays a simple D minor line in the open A minor form (*Basics 2*: Ch. 2) with a smooth distorted tone while the second, Gtr. 2, is a contrasting clean rhythm part, Rhy. Fig. 1., revealing Gilmour's R&B side. His comping is percussive and funky relying on fret-hand muting (*Basics 1*: Ch. 2), sixteenth-note strumming (*Basics 1*: Ch. 3) and syncopation (see *Power Studies 1*: "Bang A Gong") and the use of the Dm chord in open A minor form (*Basics 3*: p. 19).

In the choruses [B], three guitars play the well-conceived accompaniment parts. Gtrs. 2 and 3 use the Stratty clean tone established in the verses and Gtr. 1 plays the dirty power chords, shown in slashes—a perfect example of Gilmour's uncluttered and effective guitar orchestration strategy. Note the use of the F (*Basics 3*: p. 34) and C (*Basics 3*: p. 26) barre chords in Gtr. 1's part. Also check out the triads used in the other two guitar parts. These can easily be traced back to their open forms: the F triad is directly based on the open D form (*Basics 3*: Ch. 5) and the C triad is based on the open E form (*Basics 3*: Ch. 4). (For more on triads see *Advanced Concepts and Techniques*.)

Gilmour's solo [C] is classic— a "must-learn" for all guitarists. The insights it yields in terms of string bending and phrasing alone are extremely useful—particularly his wide string bends (1 1/2, 2 and 2 1/2 step bends) and intonation. Also noteworthy is the way he interpolates double-stop textures with single-note playing in his lines. The solo further presents a valuable study in combining the various shapes of the minor pentatonic scale in D minor. During the improvisations he moves in and out of a number of forms, beginning in the E minor "blues-box" form (*Basics 2*: Ch. 4 and *Basics 3*: Ch. 1) and continuing through the open G minor, A minor and D minor forms—see *Basics 3*: Ch. 7 for details on these connections. Check out his frequent addition of the second (or ninth), E, during the solo. This is a common expansion of the minor pentatonic scale favored by countless guitarists including Jimi Hendrix, Eric Johnson, Eric Clapton, Carlos Santana, and Stevie Ray Vaughan. (In this regard, be sure to look at "Black Magic Woman" and "Lenny" elsewhere in *Power Studies 3* for more examples.)

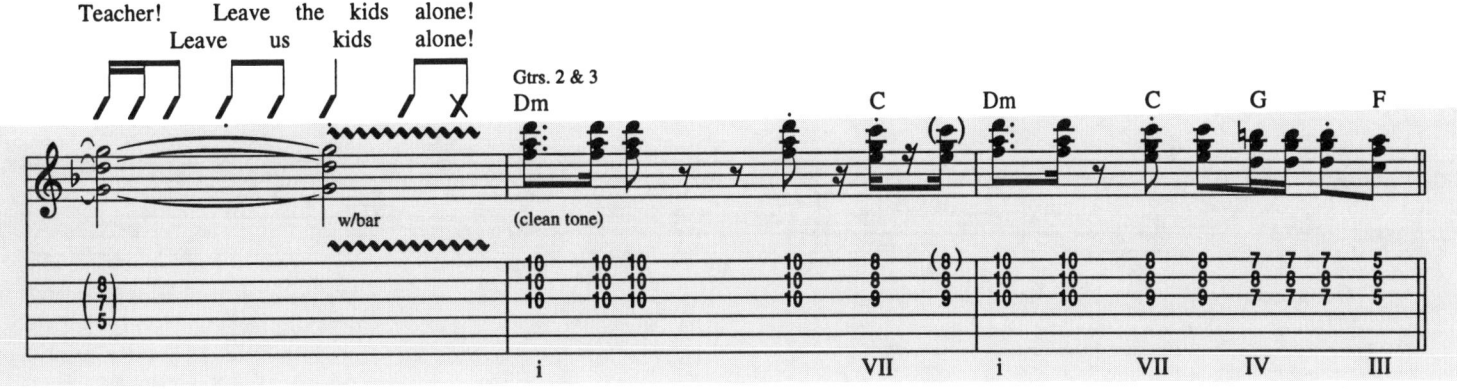

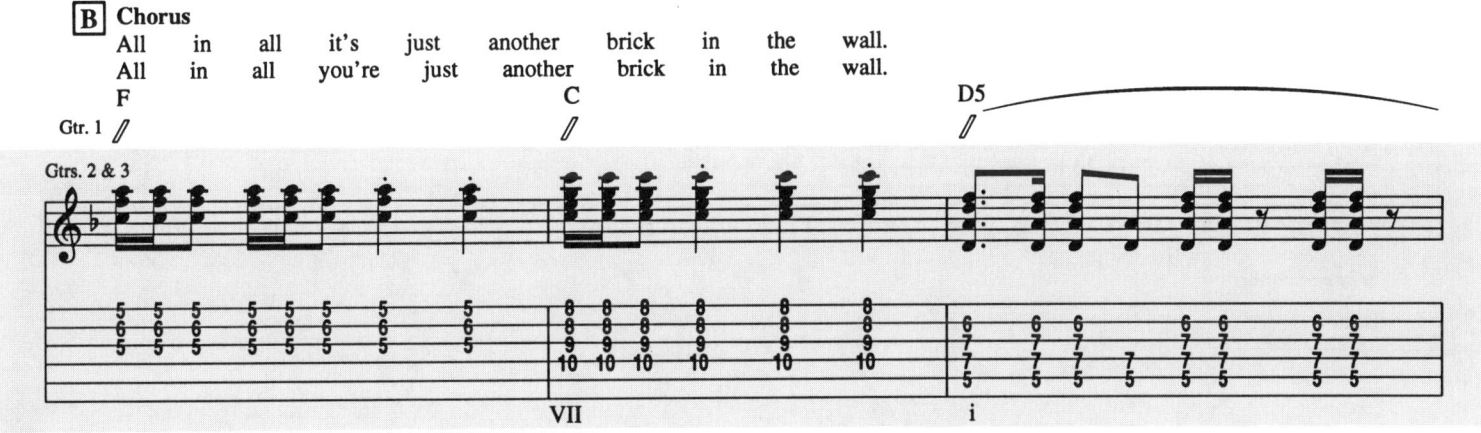

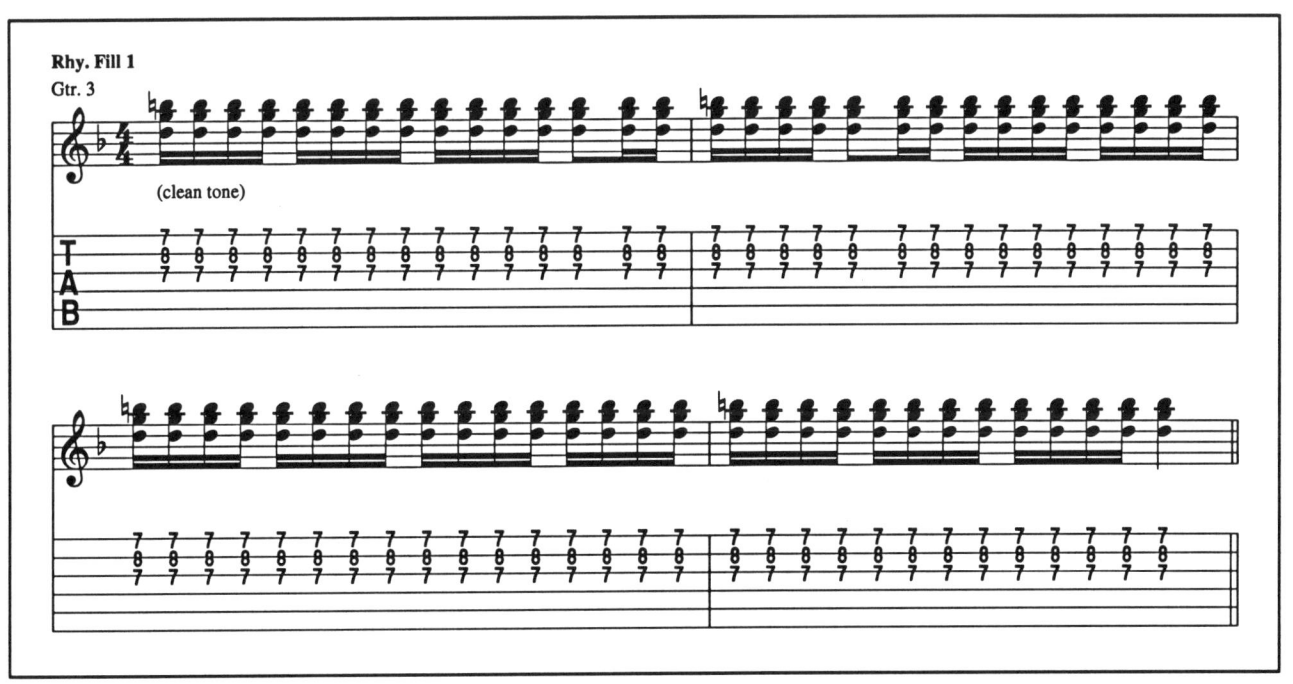

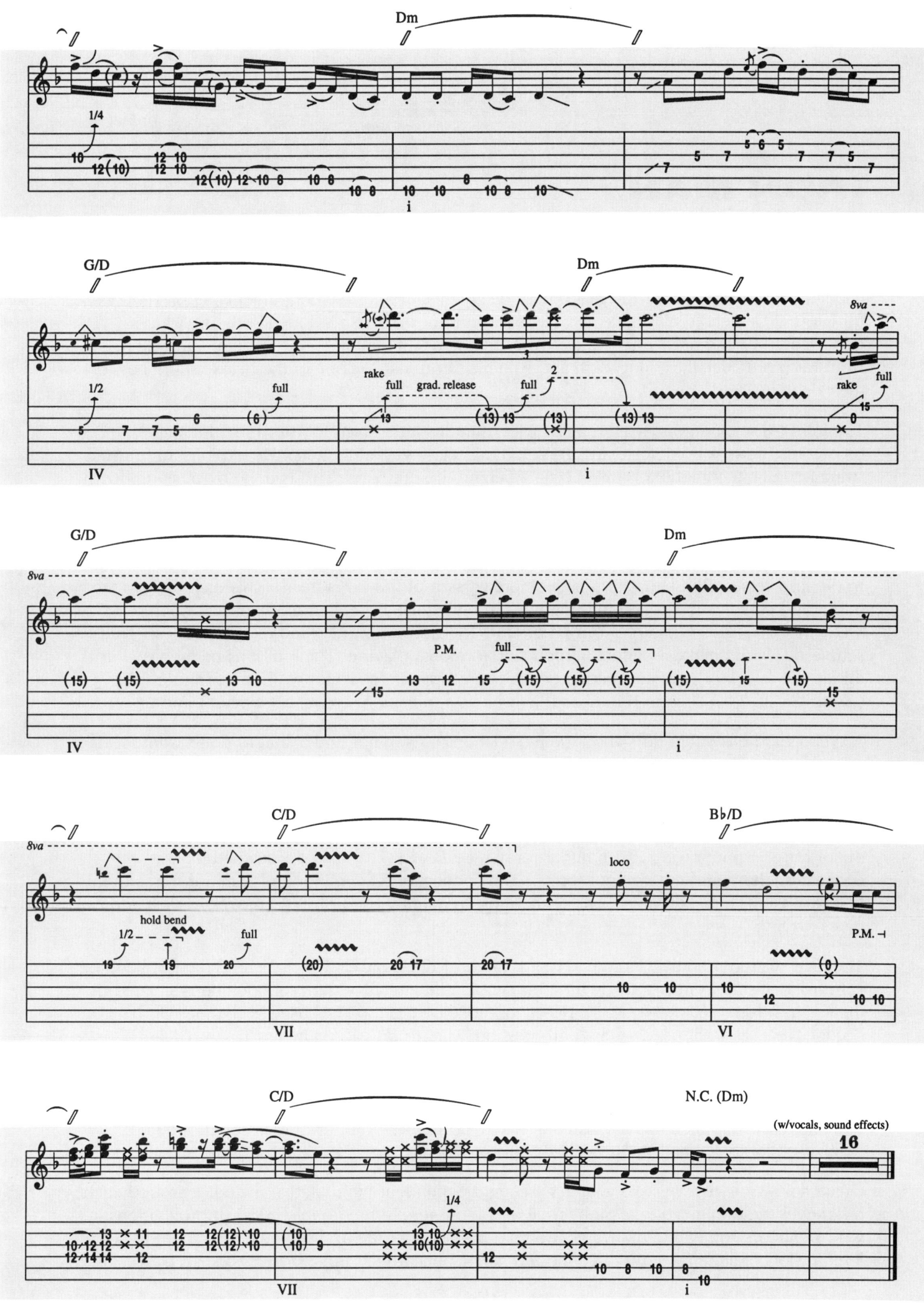

IRON MAN
Black Sabbath

Arriving with thundering riffs, sinister occult themes and dark gothic trappings, Black Sabbath is generally acknowledged as the first official heavy metal band—setting undeniable precedents for late-1970's metal renaissance as well as the current thrash/speed metal school. A fact underscored by the numerous bands that cite them as influential—Iron Maiden, Van Halen, Faith No More, Metallica, Megadeth and Pantera. "Iron Man" is one of the heaviest and best of their definitive early period.

The intro [A] sets the tone for the piece with ominous bass drum footsteps, the lunatic protagonist's mechanoid voice and Tony Iommi's eerie groaning guitar. He exploits an unusual string bending technique for this effect—a behind-the-nut bend. This is done by pushing down the low E string toward the headstock with the fingers as if they were on the fretboard. The "Iron Man" leitmotif in the intro is in B minor and is unmistakably Sabbath—a modal rhythm riff composed entirely of movable power chords. See *Basics 2*.

In the first verses [B] [C] and [E], a single-note version of the riff is heard. This melody is in B minor and contains the added minor 6th, G, implying the B Aeolian mode or natural minor scale. (See *Advanced Concepts and Techniques* for more on modes and diatonic scales.) This simple riff would make a perfect introduction to modal playing. Think of it as being based in B minor like its minor pentatonic counterpart. Seen this way, it would be in the G minor form (*Basics 3*: Ch. 7). A second B minor riff is used as a transition to connect verses 1 and 2.

A syncopated ensemble riff signals the modulation to C# minor and a shift to double-time feel establishing a new key and groove for the guitar solo. The riff's C# pentatonic melody incorporates the flat five "blue note", G, and uses A minor form (*Basics 3*: Ch. 2). Guitar solo 1 [D] provides an ideal study in combining the various positions of the minor pentatonic scale in C#. Tony plays predominately blues-based ideas and strings together a number of forms—C minor form, A minor form and E minor form. (See *Basics 3*: Ch. 7 for a detailed look at connecting these and other minor forms.) The connection of C minor and A minor forms in the first two bars is indispensable—one of the most frequently-used physical moves in rock and blues playing.

The final section modulates to the key of E minor. Here more of Tony's behind-the-nut bending is heard as well as a new melody riff. This simple and attractive minor mode line is situated in the C minor form (*Basics 3*: Ch. 7). Note that the added ninth, F#, is used in the melody. This occurs over a characteristic Sabbath progression. The progression: Em–Em/D–Em/C#–Em/C, is classically-inspired employing the harmonic technique of oblique motion. Notice that the voice-leading is in the bass line. The notes, E–D–C#–C, move down while the upper notes of the E minor chord stay put. This is the essence of oblique motion. Cultivated as a Black Sabbath trademark, they applied this harmonic device to a number of tunes in their repertoire like "Sabbath, Bloody Sabbath," "Snowblind," 'Black Sabbath" and "Looking for Today".

Guitar solo 2 [G] involves two guitars weaving independent but imitative melodies around each other over the E minor progression. There is a looseness in the double guitar improvisations which conveys something midway between a duet and a duel. In both guitar parts of this solo look for lots of shifting between connected minor pentatonic forms. (See *Basics 3*: Ch. 7.)

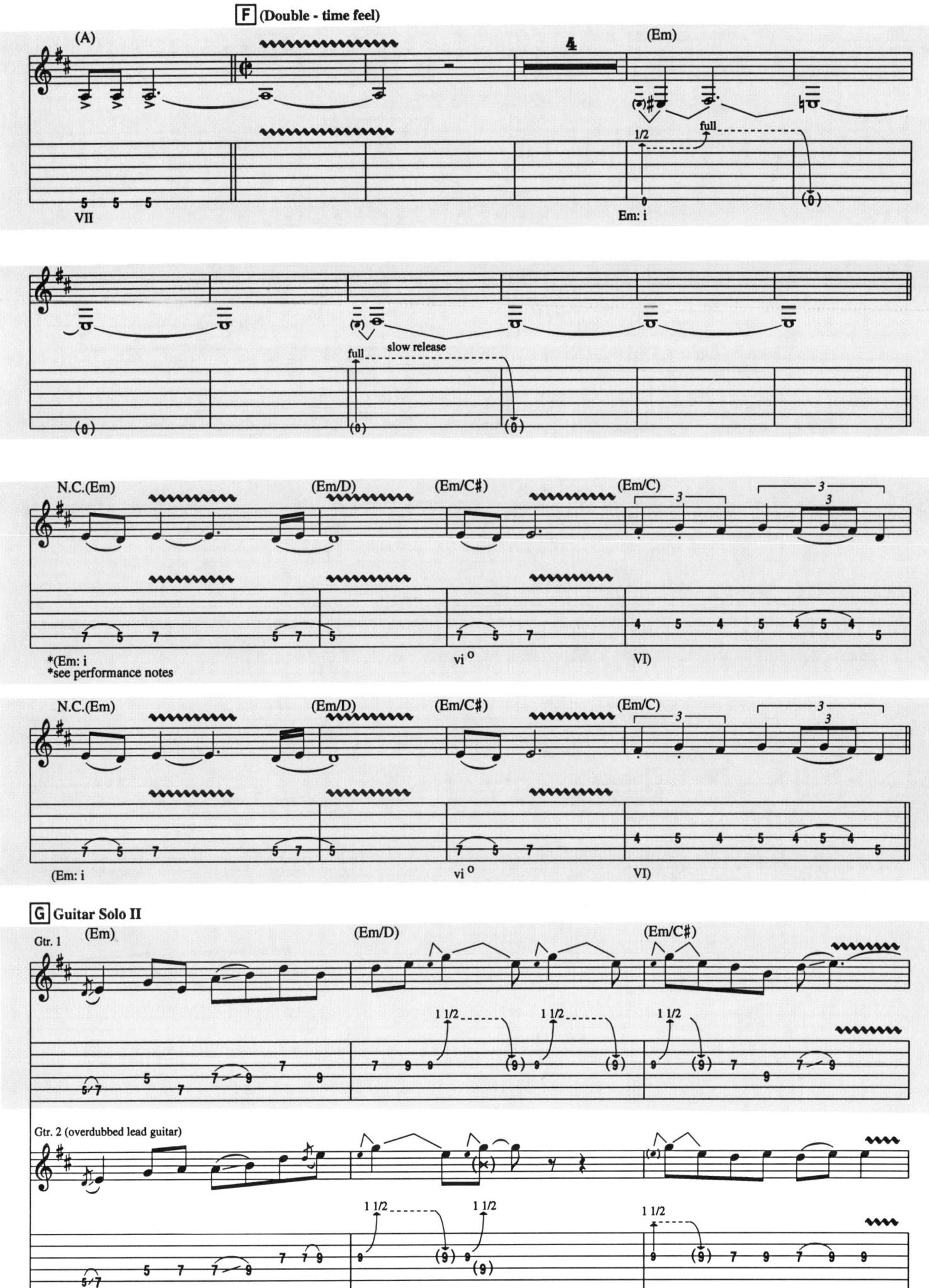

YOU SHOOK ME
Led Zeppelin

Led Zeppelin rose in 1968 from the ashes of the proto-metal Yardbirds—a group that produced the mighty British rock guitar triumvirate of Clapton, Beck and Page. Final guitarist Jimmy Page, veteran of the fertile London recording scene and heir to the legacy, fashioned what many consider to be the most important hard rock band of the 1970's during the Yardbirds' final death throes. Following the lead of Eric Clapton in Cream and the Jeff Beck Group with Rod Stewart, he steeped the powerful new band in blues classics in addition to writing extraordinary new pieces. "You Shook Me" from Zep's eponymously titled debut album is a prime example. Their take on Willie Dixon's classic presented a much heavier blues-rock attitude and sound with a plodding groove that presaged the heavy metal of the '70's, loud, aggressive guitarwork and heightened vocal-guitar interaction.

The intro [A] begins in free time with some slippery slide guitar—an early Page trademark. The band is in by the next phrase as is a definite tempo. This is a great section to work on for basic slide technique in standard tuning. The slide lines rely on simple pentatonic melody. Like jamming buddy, Eric Clapton, Page is fond of mixing of major and minor sounds and forms. You'll find E minor form (*Basics 3*: Ch. 1), G minor form (*Basics 3*: Ch. 7), G form (*Basics 3*: Ch. 1) and A minor form (*Basics 3*: Ch. 2) used in this section.

The verses [B] are marked by the heavy slow shuffle groove. Here, Page uses a simple, open-position blues comping riff played on the low E string—spartan but very powerful. The accompaniment is decorated with various slide fills in A minor form, E minor form and G minor form.

Behind the organ and harmonica solos [C] and [D], Page keeps it simple and rootsy. He develops a straightforward rhythm groove with open and movable blues comping figures. (See *Basics 1* and *Basics 2*.) It's interesting and enlightening to compare his figures with Clapton's comping and arpeggiated chords in "Ramblin' on my Mind" in *Power Studies 1*.

Page's guitar solo [E] is well-conceived, starting with understatement and restraint and building inexorably to a powerful climax. He begins with sparse but melodious slide lines. Though these are played with the slide we can still perceive them as chord-based physical shapes and as being part of our network of fretboard forms The lines fit into the E form, G form and D form (*Basics 3*: Ch. 5). The second part of the solo is more dynamic, involved and virtuosic. Page wails with notey E major pentatonic passages based on the C form (*Basics 3*: Ch. 2). Check out the B–B♭–A chromaticism he consistently adds for melodic flow. He also incorporates the minor third, G, into the phrase for that unmistakable blues-rock impression a la Clapton, Hendrix and Beck. On the B–A–E (V–IV–I) cadence, Page continues mixing minor and major sounds more vigorously. Here, he uses the D minor form (*Basics 3*: Ch. 4), E minor form, G form and A minor form.

In the outro [F], the tempo reverts to free time. Page plays out of the D minor form and C minor form (*Basics 3*: Ch. 7) during the infamous Page/Plant guitar/vocal interplay.

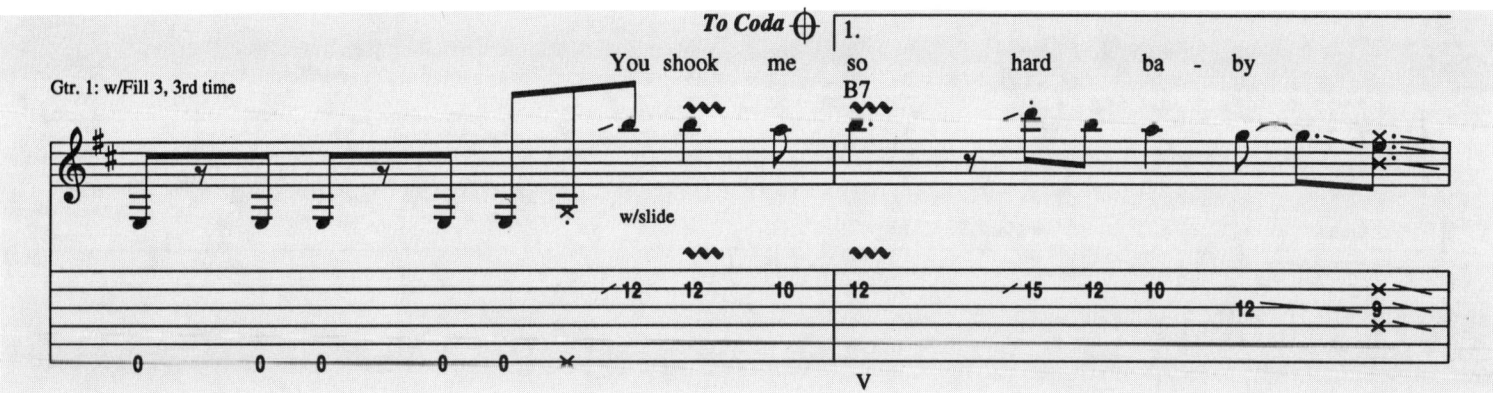
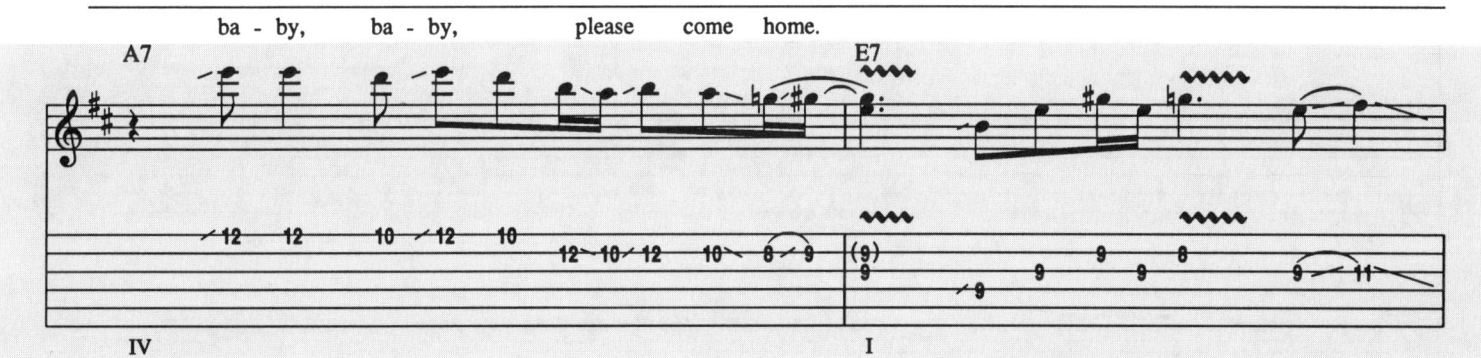

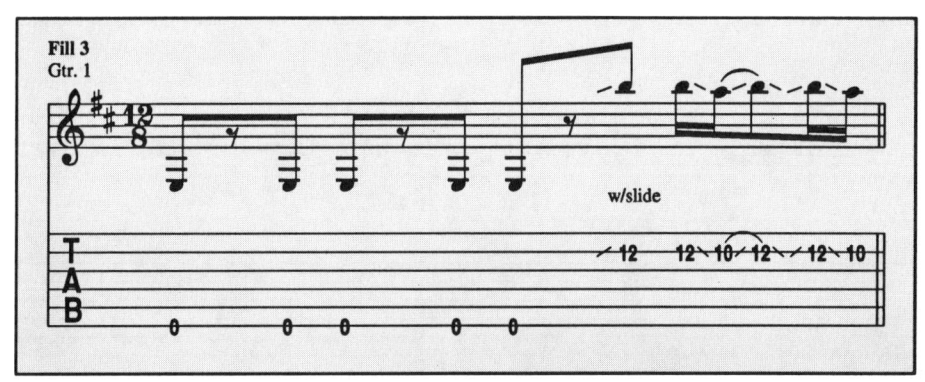

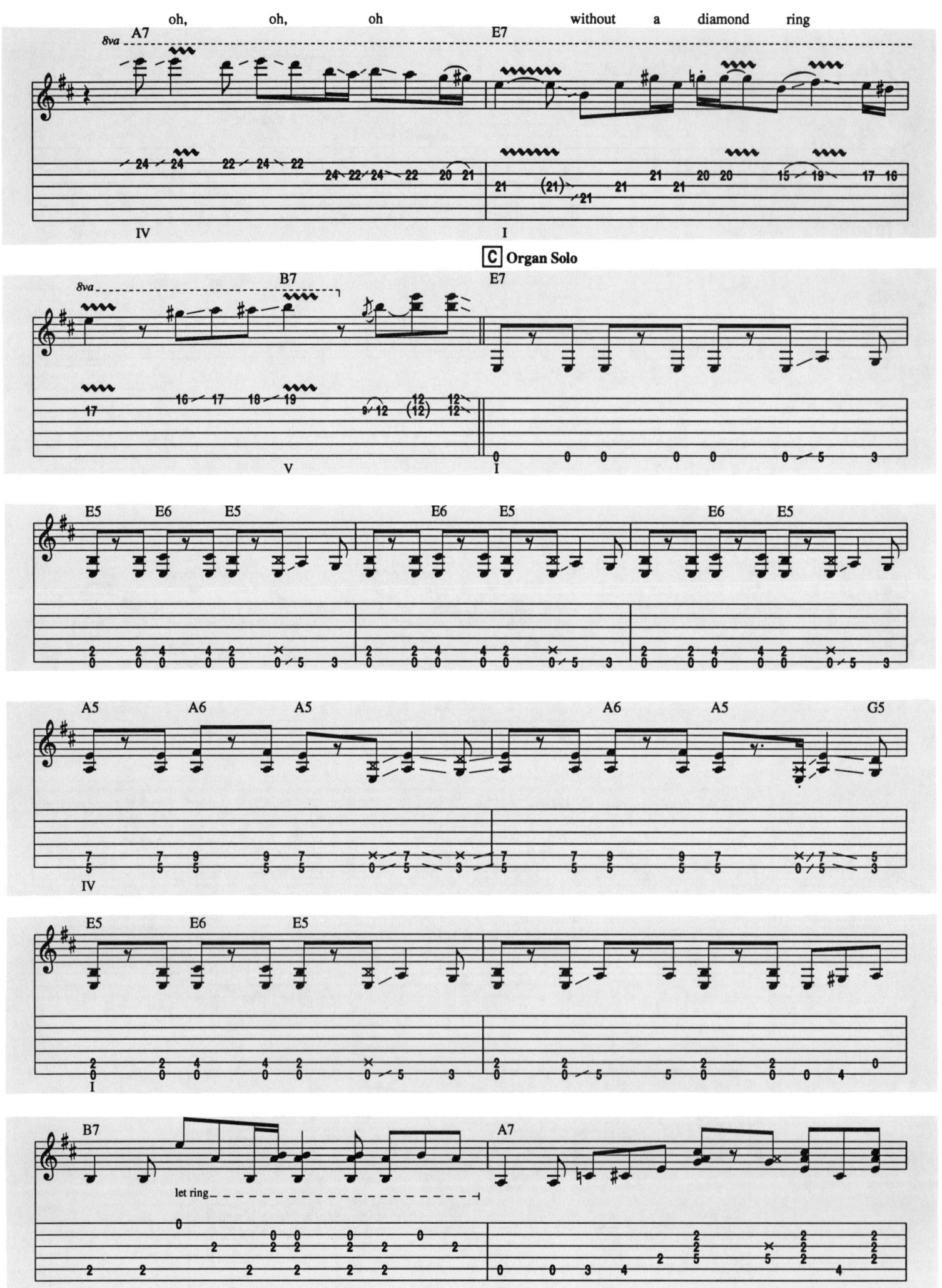

E7
Gtr. 2: w/Fill 1
B
E Guitar Solo
E5 E6 E7 E5 E7 E6 E5 E7/D Am/C E A G
Gtr. 1
Gtr. 2
8va
w/slide
w/o slide
E/B A/C# E/B A G E7type2 E5
wo/slide
*w/octave - above effect
A5
full

Fill 1
Gtr. 2 (overdubbed)
w/slide
w/o slide
(Distortion w/echo & reverb)

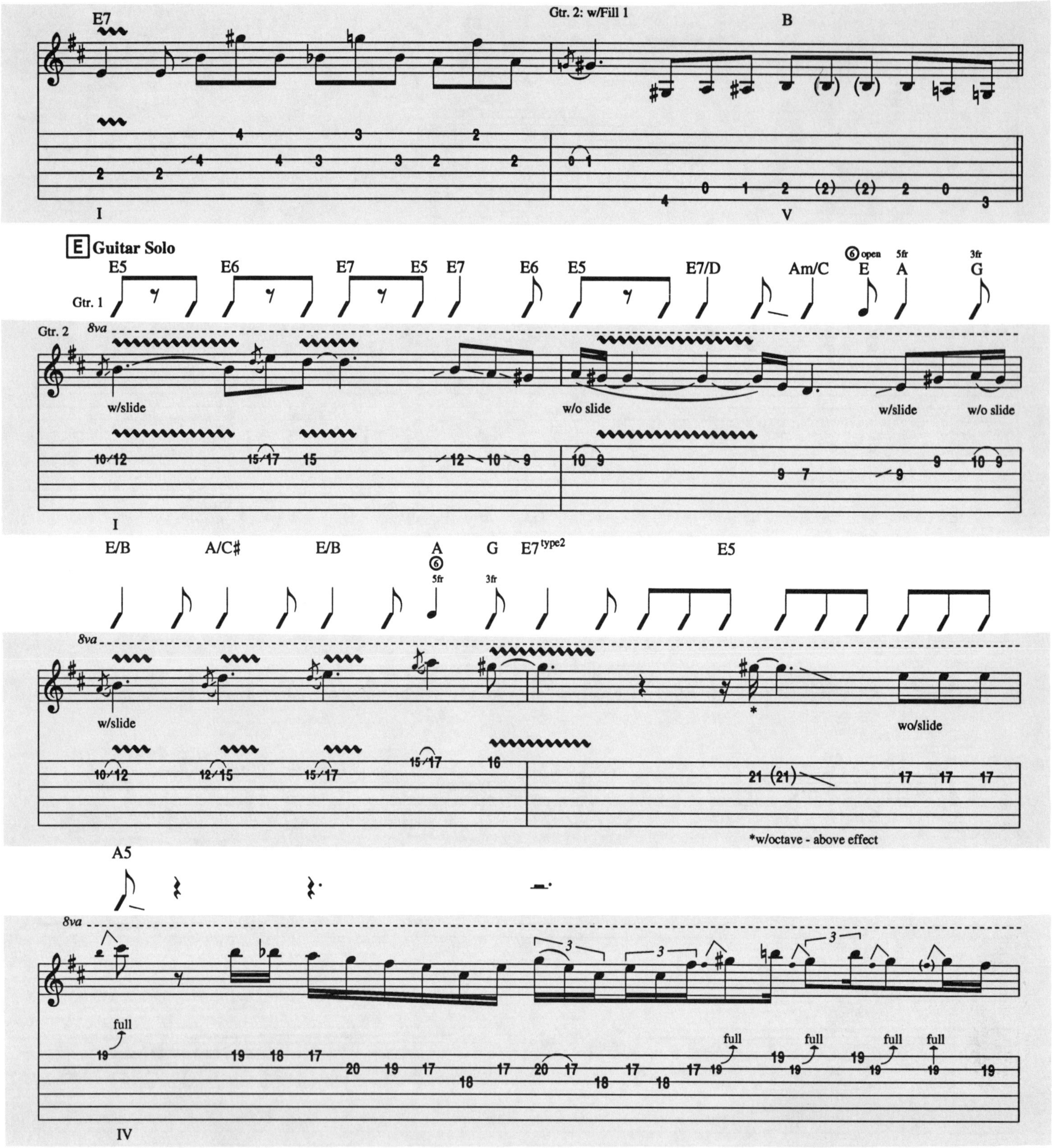

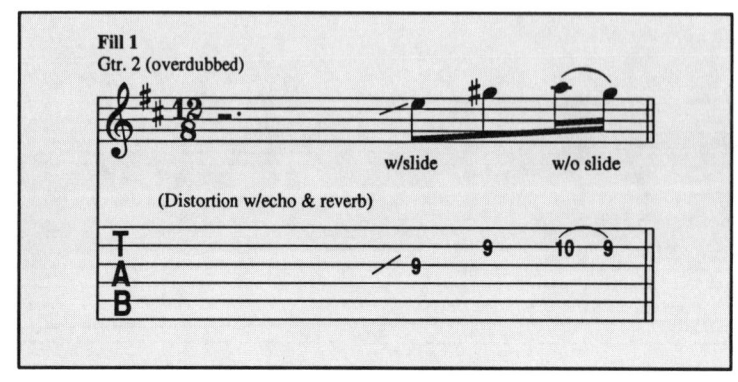

8va
full
Gtr. 1: w/Rhy. Fill 1
E
Gtr. 2
I
B7
V
Rhy. Fill 1
Gtr. 1
let ring
1/2

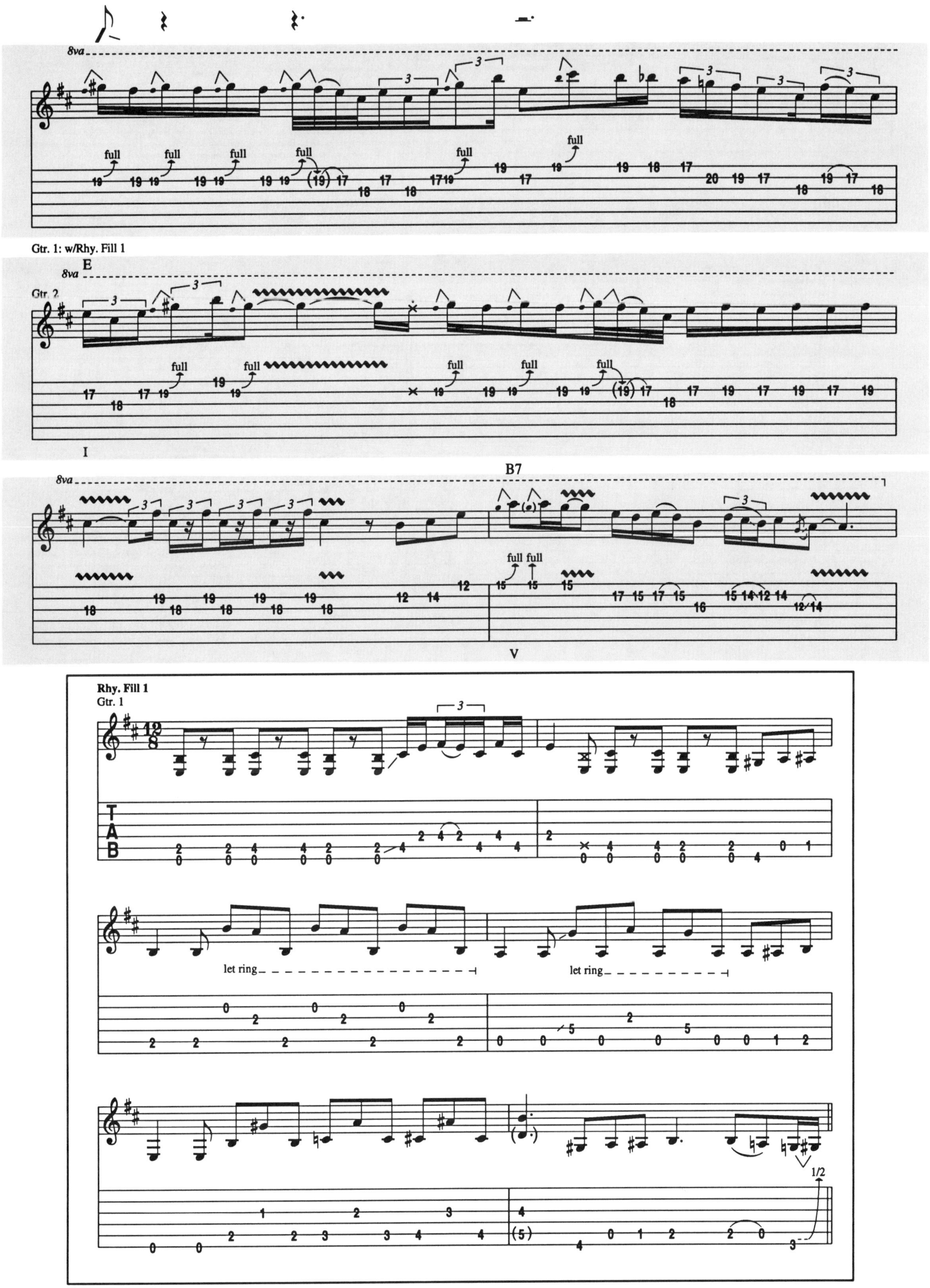

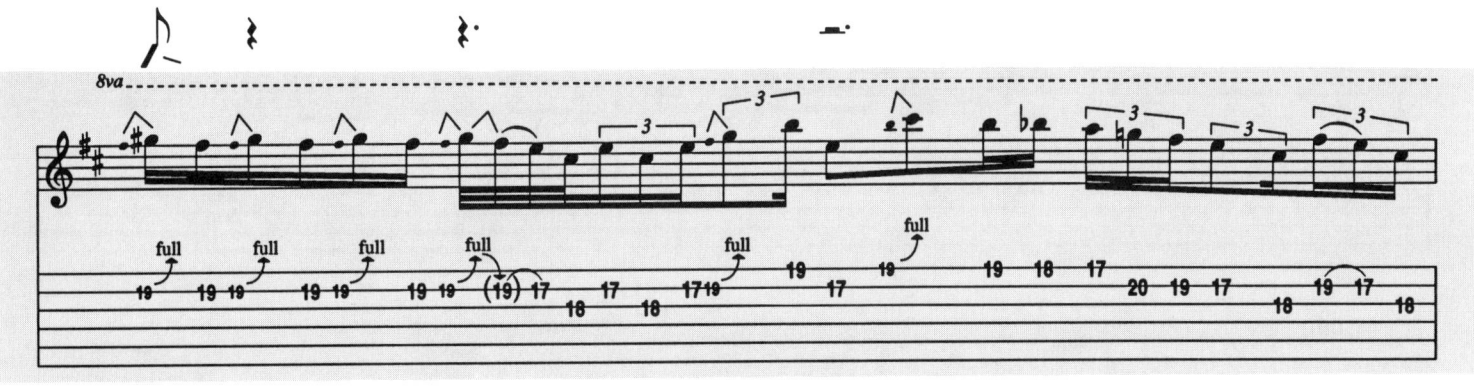

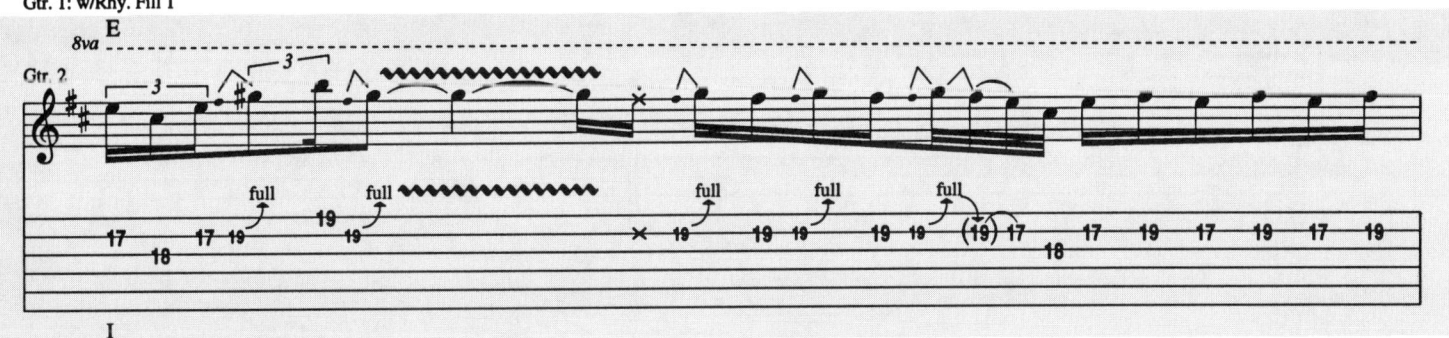

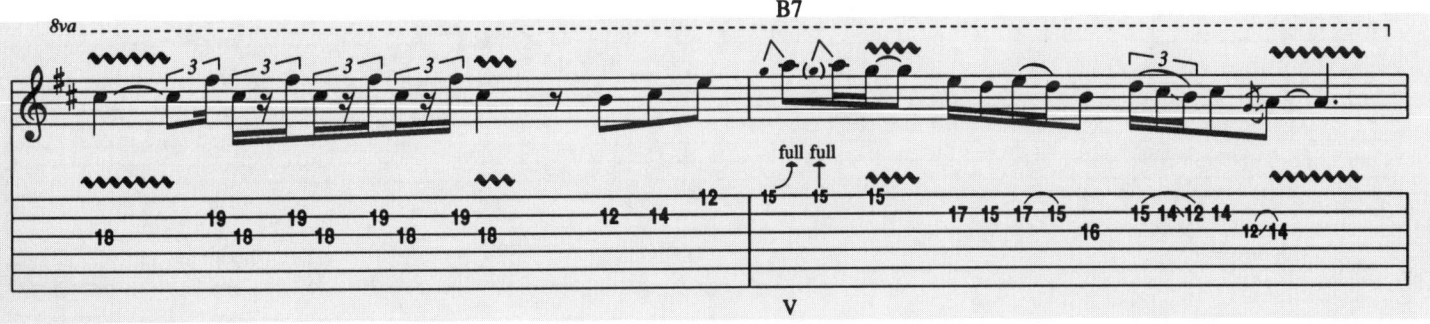

Additional Lyrics

2. I have a bird that whistles and
   I have birds that sing.
   I have a bird that whistles and
   I have birds that sing.
   I have a bird won't do nothin; oh, oh, oh, oh,
   without a diamond ring.

3. You know you shook me, babe,
   You shook me all night long.
   I know you really, really did, babe.
   I think you shook me, baby,
   You shook me all night long.
   You shook me so hard, baby, I know. *(Outro)*

GLOSSARY

There are a number of important and useful musical terms, abbreviations and stylistic elements found in modern guitar transcriptions and arrangements. So that it will be easier for you to negotiate your way through the Power Studies songs, the following list and explanations are offered.

1. RIFF. In a general sense, this is synonymous with repeated figure. A riff is normally a self-contained and sonically identifiable musical idea. In a song form sense, it has a more specific meaning. It means a recurring figure or pattern which is structurally important to the arrangement. It is used to describe a mostly single-note figure or one that is more melodic than chordal. Multiple riffs in a song are given letter names to distinguish one from the other. For example, Riff A, Riff B, Riff C and so on. It is named when it first appears so that it may be recalled throughout the arrangement.

2. RHYTHM FIGURE. This is the converse of riff. Rhythm Figure refers to a recurring pattern which is more chordal than melodic. It can be a purely strummed part, a series of arpeggiated chords, triads, an intricate progression or something as simple as just a repeating diad. Multiple rhythm figures in a song are abbreviated and given numbers in an arrangement. For example, Rhy. Fig. 1, Rhy. Fig. 2 and so on.

3. TACET. This means don't play in a particular section of a song. When you have several bars of tacet, it is written as long, thick whole-note rest with brackets on each end. The number above the rest tells you how many measures to remain silent.

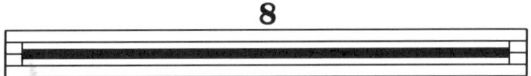

4. GUITARS. In arrangements with more than one guitar, they are given proper guitar part names, abbreviated and numbered. For example, Gtr. 1, Gtr. 2, etc. If there is something significant about the particular Gtr. part it will usually be cited. For example, acoustic or electric guitar, clean, semi-clean (semi-cln.) or distorted (dirty) tone, etc. Particular articulations are also cited: let ring, P.M., with fingers and pick, with slide, etc. Effects which significantly process the sound are similarly designated: with echo, with fuzz, with flanger, etc.

5. SONG FORM. Here are some basic musical symbols, terms and points used to set up the structure of a song as an arrangement.

REPEAT MARKS. These are written as bracketed sections with thick barlines on the outside and thin barlines on the inside. These are followed by two vertical dots. If they are repeated more than once, the direction is written as a number of times. For example, these symbols

mean repeat the inside two bars (play them twice) and then continue. If you played them again (three times) it would be written with this added direction

Play 3 times

First, second, third (etc.) endings are used with longer repeat sections if their final few bars have different music. For example these symbols

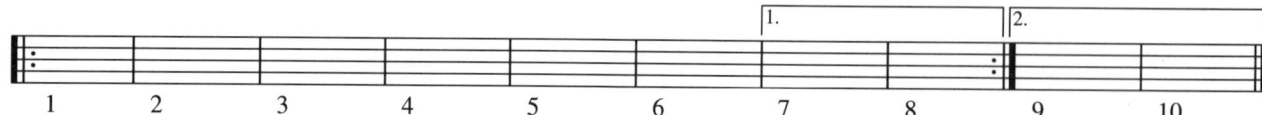

mean that you are dealing with an eight bar section which has different music in the last two bars on the repeat. Play the first eight bars (1-8), repeat only the first six bars (1-6) before going on to the second ending (bars 9-10) to complete the eight-bar section.

D.S. (DAL SEGNO). This literally means "from the sign". You'll see it accompanied by this symbol: 𝄋

It is used to indicate the beginning of a section to be repeated. The abbreviation D.S. means go to the sign and repeat until a new direction is given or until the music ends. D.S. is usually found with the words Al Coda. And no, Al Coda is not a famous Italian musician. D.S. Al Coda means "from the sign, go to the coda".

CODA. This literally means "the tail" and refers to a concluding section of a piece of music. You'll see it written with this symbol: ⊕

Inside these broad mappings of the arrangement, you will find the various song form sections labelled. These could include:

INTRO (Introduction). VERSES (1st Verse, 2nd Verse, etc.). PRE-CHORUS. CHORUS. INTERLUDE. BRIDGE. SOLO (or solos). OUTRO (ending section).

6. FILL. This is a brief melodic figure inserted into the arrangement. These are often boxed, named and numbered. For example, Fill 1, Fill 2, etc. When these are brought into the song they are called up by the direction: w/Fill 1, w/Fill 2, etc.

7. RHYTHM FILL. This is a chordal version of the Fill. It can be an independent little figure or a piece of a larger Rhy. Fig. These are also boxed, named and numbered. When named they are abbreviated. For example, Rhy. Fill 1, Rhy. Fill 2, etc. They are called up just like Fills, by the direction: w/Rhy. Fill 1, w/Rhy. Fill 2, etc.

8. RHYTHM SLASHES. These are strum symbols written as rhythm patterns with chord names located above the staff. When you see these, look for corresponding chord frames in the beginning of the arrangement. Find the name that goes with the frame. They will show you, in diagram form, the chords to be played. For example, this

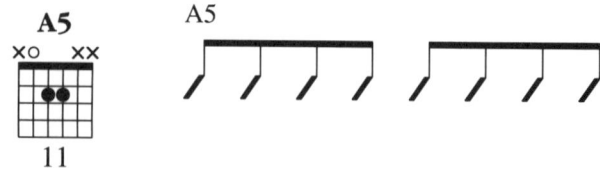

means you play the A5 chord shown in the frame with a steady eighth-note strum. Articulations like P.M. and x's are often included and appear below the rhythm pattern. Rhythm slashes can also indicate single notes in a figure. In this case, the rhythm pattern will show note heads instead of strum slashes. The note name will appear above rhythm pattern, followed by its fret number and string number.